# Living With
# Body Dysmorphic Disorder

Lea Walker

&

Janet Lee

First published in 2008
This paperback edition published in 2016 by
**Apex Publishing Ltd**
12A St. John's Road, Clacton on Sea
Essex, CO15 4BP, United Kingdom
www.apexpublishing.co.uk

Typography and layout of this edition by
Andrews UK Limited
www.andrewsuk.com

Editor: Kim Kimber
Production Manager: Chris Cowlin
Cover Design: Siobhan Smith

*For my mum and H, Jade, Jane and Richard. And
to all the people out there with good hearts.*

Lea Walker


*Dedicated to Alex Lee, my partner/soul mate for 26
years, for his unwavering support and humour.*

Janet Lee

# Contents

# Living with BDD

# My Life as a Little Girl

What was it Forrest Gump said? "Life is like a box of chocolates."

To me, well no it's not. It's like a pint of milk.

One day it's OK, the next it's like cat sick in a bottle.

I should have been a poet don't you think?

In my book I'll be touching on a few issues – like bullying, weight gain and weight loss, abusive relationships, cosmetic surgery – and of course body dysmorphic disorder (BDD).

I hope when you read this book that you find the determination to just say 'fuck it, I'm going to live my life for me and nobody else' – because you don't ever have to be what you don't want to be.

You will, and can be, happy no matter what. But you do have to take control – and you will, because you are strong enough to do it.

This isn't an autobiography as such.

I'm writing this book (well some of it as I'm not the brightest of sparks – so I'm having someone help me) with the hope of giving you an insight into the day-to-day life of a sufferer of BDD, which looking back I have had from the age of about six.

I wanted to try and write it myself so it's coming from my heart and no one else can do that.

Body dysmorphic disorder is a self-hatred, a loathing of yourself – pretty shite actually if you happen to be a sufferer.

Even if you are not a sufferer I guarantee you will know someone who is.

I was born on 11th September, 1970 in Nottingham to my mum Doreen and me dad Cliff.

I'm the youngest of four. My eldest brother's name is Kevin

who is 21 years older than me, then Robert (20 years older), and Darryl (five years older).

Me poor mam was 40 when she had me and thought she was in her 'change' (menopause for those of you who don't know what that is).

Christ, what a shock, thinking you're in the change and then you give birth.

But to make it even worse for me poor mam and dad, she gave birth to me.

I'm not just saying this, but God almighty I was one UGLY baby. I'd say it was a mix up between me and the placenta, and the placenta was nicer to look at, but they threw the wrong one away.

My dad wanted to call me Donna Michelle.

But no, my bloody brother Darryl wanted to call me Lisa Michelle. So of course, that's what I got called. So thanks broth' for that one.

When I was a little girl my Mammar and Gang Gang (my grandparents) called me Lealea and I liked that, so kept it instead of Lisa.

I always associate the name Lisa as being in trouble because that's what my dad would shout.

"Lisa! Get in here!"

Or "Lisa! Get down these bleeding stairs NOW!"

Or I associate the name with my teachers shouting.

"Lisa! Are you stupid?"

Or "Lisa! Stand in the corner!"

"Lisa! Hands out!" Which meant either a ruler or cane and sometimes a slipper.

Now can you see why I'm not too keen on that name?

Guess I'm going to have to start at the beginning with my dad, who I feel in some ways has made me the person I am today. It's appropriate I start right back with the man who has turned me into me, craving the love of a man, which never happened.

If I had had the love of my dad, the cuddles and kisses, then I personally don't think I would be the person I am today: craving love, wanting to be accepted, wanting to be made a fuss of, wanting to be told I am not a bad person – and finding it difficult to be with a straight man.

So here I go...

My dad Cliff was in the navy from the age of 15. When he left the navy he became a miner in Nottingham. He worked at all different pits: Babbington, Newstead, Calverton and Gedling. He did work bloody hard though.

We lived on a pit road in a pit house. We weren't brought up in squalor but we didn't have much money at all and were looked down on in the area even though our home was quite nice.

We didn't have much, but we were grateful for what we had. I didn't have everything I would have liked, but dad did his best working on the pit face.

The north is famous for its lace, textiles, fishermen, docklands and mining industry. But miners were paid a quarter of the wages of those working in other industries.

Perhaps that's why us northerners think differently and are a lot harder than other folk. They are grateful for what they have and don't take things for granted. A lot of us northerners have been dragged up; but I have never met a weak northern person because they are more likely to be told: "Now stop it. Pull yourself together, pack it in."

But I've met a lot of weak southerners. Northern folk are certainly not given as much as those in the south when it comes to job opportunities and pay, but we all have good hearts.

Despite their difficulties mum and dad still managed to buy their pit house.

A lot of my friends grew up in bigger houses and went on holidays abroad. But we could never afford that. But we would be content with a break in a caravan or at Butlins.

My mum is Doreen. She used to be called 'the Duchess' by people on our road because she looked so beautiful. We lived in a pit house, and most of the wives looked like pit wives, but my mum looked really posh because she was so beautiful; she looked just like Grace Kelly or Liz Taylor.

Everyone else called her 'Doo Doo'.

I wouldn't say my brothers were notorious, but they had a reputation for being fighters and took no messing from anyone. They were brought up in the 1950s and '60s – the era of mods and rockers.

Like my mum and dad, my brothers could always look after themselves – and they protected others.

I can remember when I was a little girl, one of my first memories was the 'nougat man' who used to be at the top of the hill where we lived every weekend, ringing a bell and selling 2p worth of nougats to us kids.

In Nottingham we always have the 'Goose Fair', a travelling fair which visits every October.

I can clearly remember coming home from the fair when I was about five or six to the terrible shock of dad sitting in his chair covered in blood. His head had been crushed, his teeth pushed through his lip and he was covered in stitches. Dad was a mess. Loads of neighbours were there and mum was crying.

Dad had been in a pit accident and been trapped underground when the mine collapsed.

He had saved a neighbour's life in the accident.

But it broke my heart to see him looking like that and to see mum in tears.

I remember going to infant school crying and telling my teacher Mrs Burrows (who was like a second mum to me) that I was frightened daddy was going to die.

Pits were collapsing all the time and dad was involved in many accidents.

But he had a family to support, so he went back to work and mum took a cleaning job in the main offices of Esso. Me and my brother Darryl stayed at Mama and Gang Gang's.

On school holidays I used to love it when dad took us to the pit to collect his wages on a Friday.

Dad would take me and Darryl for a cup of tea and a bacon sandwich with tomato sauce at the pit cafeteria. I would have fried bread in drippin' – yuk! That would be the highlight of our week.

Me and Darryl would sit in the changing rooms where the miners would strip off when they came out of the pit. They were walking round with pitch black faces and white bums, completely stark naked!

Christ Almighty! Can you imagine that happening nowadays?

They were just the happiest days: school holidays and spending time with my dad and going to the pit.

I remember being really upset when dad wouldn't let me go with him once as punishment for being naughty.

I sat at home with mum eating celery soup and dried bread – thinking of my brother eating his bacon sandwich (though I don't eat meat any more. The thought of eating meat nowadays makes me feel physically sick).

I was devastated that my dad took Darryl and didn't take me. I was jealous because my brother had gone and he would be spending time with my dad while I was stuck at home. Dad wasn't around much, so whatever time we did have I used to like spending it with him.

I know dad loved us. He loved my mum, he really did, but he had a lot of affairs. My mum just wasn't dad's soul mate – though my dad might have been mum's. You can love people in a different way or you can love them properly and be 'in love' with them.

You can love people because they are part of you when you are growing up.

Sometimes mum and dad would fall out, usually because dad might have had another woman. It used to break my heart. The worse thing for me was to see my mum cry.

But dad was not happy and he was looking for happiness.

Unfortunately my mum had to suffer. But you can't make someone else's life a misery just to make yourself happy.

Me and Darryl would often cry when mum and dad would argue when we were really little. Our two older brothers had left home so it didn't affect them as much.

But despite the problems at home, overall I think I was lucky growing up in the '70s.

I was surrounded by fields. It seemed that when it was spring, it really was spring. I loved it when the flowers came through. And in the infants school we would have a Maypole dance and Easter bonnet parades. I would make bonnets with my mum and we would boil eggs and decorate them.

And when it was summer, you really knew it was summer. During the six week summer holidays it was always baking hot. Even when it rained it was still hot. There would be pollen, grasses and dandelion seeds blowing from the fields. It would even smell like summer. I loved sitting on 'the rec' with my ice cream.

Even as a child I loved the changes, whether it was lovely springs, baking hot summers which lasted for months, heavy rain or freezing cold.

And Christmas was really Christmas, not like it is today, which is such a shame.

Back then Christmas started a week before 25th December – not like now when festive displays are in the stores from September – and by January Easter eggs are already in the shops.

Mum and dad would take us Christmas shopping

Christmas in the '70s meant the nativity play at school (which I was never included in). I always wanted to be in it, but I never had the nerve because I was too shy, too self-conscious.

Looking back, our home was a complete fire hazard: mum and dad smoking that many fags, paper chains round the walls held up by drawing pins, Christmas cards hanging up and glittery lanterns on the ceiling.

But everything is so commercialised now. I know things have to move forward, but it would be nice to keep some sort of tradition.

Our holidays would be at Pontin's or Butlins where I would have the excitement of entering competitions, taking part in a donkey derby, and watching a dancer or comedian on the stage. I would be in the huge holiday canteen having dinner with mum and dad and all the other families. It was just nice to be in a holiday camp with other happy families, all laughing and joking, everyone in the same boat. None of us had much money so there was no pretence, no airs and graces – not like now when people want the best of stuff and look down their noses at you if you're not as rich as them.

Kids today have no idea what any of that was about.

I would love riding my bike to Colwick Park.

And I used to love horse riding. Dad would give me a pound for washing the car or mowing the lawns so that I could go riding. Yep – a pound. Christ, I am bloody old! To me there was nothing better than the weather being red hot, and going to the stables with my friends, galloping up and down at the side of the river, with not a care in the world.

Nobody gives you a rule about being a good parent, so mum and dad just brought us up as they saw fit. And we were never lazy kids. We all did chores.

Mum and dad always let me have my pets. There is nothing better than having something you love and cuddle, knowing it will love you back unconditionally.

I used to love my big, fat, old tabby cat Mindy who I would dress up in dolls' clothes – and she used to love it, well, to me she did. Guess she hated it really 'cos she was a cat – woops! Mindy used to sleep in my knicker drawer and chuck 'em all over!

I remember we visited the annual Hog Fair at Standhill Park, Carlton. Mum had cooked a chicken. She noticed Mindy was asleep on her bed in the lounge, but she locked her out of the kitchen and left the chicken out on the breakfast bar for when we got back.

But of course Mindy somehow got into the kitchen, savaged the chicken to an inch of its life and dragged it to her bed! She was such a little bleeder, a little sod, but I loved that little pussy cat so much.

She died when I was about six or seven and I felt I had lost my little friend. Mum and dad would pick me up from infants school and one day when they came to meet me, they told me Mindy had been put down as she had cancer. I was so upset I got Snowy my rabbit out of his hutch and he stayed in my bedroom all night.

When you are little you don't understand how things affect you later in life. Losing a pet is like losing part of your life, and even when you are little you can feel so empty.

We always had a cat when we were growing up.

I used to love going to my Aunty Ivy's (my grandmother's sister). There was a chip shop across the road, and every Saturday when we visited she would always give me 50p to get a bag of chips.

Ivy's house was massive with different bedrooms – and a downstairs toilet. It had a cloakroom door which to me was like the entrance to Narnia in The Lion, The Witch and The Wardrobe; and the garden was like The Secret Garden on a split level with four separate sections to rampage in. There was also a swing and apple trees.

I loved my Aunty Ivy so much. She used to make me really happy and safe.

She had a huge old tortoise, called Tommy Tortoise, who used to live in a little brick cage in the top section of the garden. I used to feed him with tomatoes. Tommy Tortoise loved free running, but he never used to go anywhere.

We would watch Worzel Gummidge on TV at Aunty Ivy's on a Sunday afternoon. She would do a piklet and a cup of Horlicks and she had a red soda syphon which she would let me squirt into her glass of booze. She had a Yorkshire terrier called Cilla who had long fur that covered her eyes, so I used to put it in a pony tail with a red ribbon.

Aunty Ivy had a male friend called Jackie who had a horse, Minstrel. He used to ride it from Colwick Park along Valley Road to Aunty Ivy's. He was massive, like a big old dray horse. I used to love trotting round Aunty Ivy's garden or Carlton 'Rec' on Minstrel.

I used to hear Aunty Ivy telling mum to leave my dad, but I couldn't understand why, being so young.

When I was eight dad moved out after a huge argument with mum and went to live in a flat. She found out he was seeing another woman, so he left. Unfortunately, at this time mum had to have a hip operation, so she asked Mama and Gang Gang to look after me and Darryl while she was in hospital. But because we were so young they couldn't cope and my grandad was working.

So dad moved back in with us.

While mum was in hospital having her operation they used a certain instrument in the theatre for cauterising the wound to stop bleeding. But one of the staff had rested the hot instrument on the bottom of her back/at the top of the cheek of her bum by mistake while she was under the anaesthetic.

Because mum was out of it she didn't know, but it was actually burning through her skin.

When we went to visit mum in hospital she was in a mess, badly scarred. Poor mum was lying on her stomach screaming in agony. I was so upset. Dad was devastated and crying. Mum still has a scar from that incident today. Pity there wasn't where there's a blame there's a claim in them days innit?

We came back home from visiting mum is hospital – and that was the only time I really felt my dad liked me.

It was the first time we ever had a Chinese meal. I remember he bought Darryl a pancake roll, but he threw it away because he didn't like it. I had king prawn fried rice. I ate the prawns, but threw the rice away. We got a right bollocking when dad found the food in the dustbin.

I couldn't sleep so dad let me sleep in his bed. We were watching a horror film called Theatre of Blood in bed. It starred Vincent Price and it was the first horror film I had ever seen. There was a bit where there was a plastic sheet and a man being butchered. I fell asleep clinging on to my dad for dear life and he was hugging me.

When I look back, all my friends were a couple of years older than me. When I was seven I used to think my really good friend was beautiful. Because I was such an ugly child I used to look at my mates and think 'why can't I be like them?'

I used to be bullied at school because people would find out about my dad's affairs. The kids would call me all the names under the sun.

Dad used to drive around the area in the car with one of his knockoffs, so everyone would know that he had a new woman on the go. One of the women only lived at the top of the road. All the miners lived in the area and they had kids, so they all knew.

"Your dad's shagging so and so," they'd say.

Or: "Your dad doesn't love your mum."

Or: "Your mum and dad don't love you."

"You stink because you're poor."

"You're from a pit house."

I think that is why I made friends with people who had even less than me.

My house was never scruffy – and it never smelled.

But I would go to houses of friends that did. They were the kids that were picked on at school, bullied, for being smelly. But they were my friends. If they were dirty and smelly it didn't matter to me.

I was envious about one particular girl, really jealous.

She was so beautiful. Her mum and dad always used to cuddle her, which I didn't get when I was little. Her mum and dad loved each other and never used to shout at each other. When I went round their house there was never an argument.

At our house we could always watch what we wanted on TV.

So I when I slept over at her house I was surprised we weren't allowed to watch Grange Hill.

I also noticed that her dad hadn't gone out.

"When does your dad go out?" I asked. "Hasn't he got a girlfriend?"

"My dad doesn't go out without my mum," she said.

It was then I wondered why my dad had to go out and mum stay in.

At my house, every Friday night when dad had gone out and left us again, mum would treat me and Darryl to a bar of chocolate before we sat down to watch TV.

We would sit watching The Rag Trade, Morecambe and Wise, Citizen Smith, The Liver Birds and Coronation Street.

Every Sunday night mum would make us salmon and cucumber sandwiches and we would have our tea listening to the charts. We would tape the charts and write down the words so we could sing them and make up dance routines. Then it was bath time.

Then dad would let us watch That's Life with Esther Rantzen before bed.

By Sunday teatime I was already frightened and scared, because I knew it wouldn't be long before dad would say 'time for bed' and it would be Monday morning again soon.

Dad would make us switch the lights off when we went to bed and I would lie there so frightened wondering whether I would be hurt, spat on as I walked up the donkey steps, or made to cry the following day at school.

Even today I have vivid memories of this – even 30 odd years on I still feel shaky sometimes remembering back to how Sunday night used to make me feel. Being so young and so scared – it was awful.

The donkey steps were in an area like an orchard, called Back Fields where 'Mad Jack' used to live in a huge house. There were always stories going round about how he murdered his wife and kids and buried them in the garden, so it used to be a dare to go scrumping in his garden. We called it 'Mad Jack's', but its proper name was Back Fields. There were apple, damson and plum trees there so some of the kids would pelt me with rotten apples or rub them into my hair.

I really wanted to be able to tell my mum what was going on, but didn't know how.

I loved learning and some of the teachers, but I hated school. Sometimes when we went to bed mum would sit crying because she would know that dad was with his other woman. Me and Darryl would always know when dad had someone else.

But when I was a teenager I was devastated to find out one of the women was someone I had known affectionately as my Aunty Carol for years.

Mum told me later in life: "She's not your bloody Aunty Carol she was one of your dad's knockoffs."

Aunty Carol – who used to buy me dollies.

One of my mum's best friends. That was one big shock. I really thought she was my aunty. It really did mess my head up a lot to find out it had all been a lie, a complete farce. I used to go and visit my 'aunty'. To find out it was all bullshit really hurt.

I think the problem with my dad was he was so handsome, and looking back I suppose he was a catch to most women.

But me mam was stunning and my brothers are gorgeous. My brother Robert had the look of an angel.

My brothers are all well over 6 ft. They took after my Gang Gang's side.

Gang Gang was 6ft 7in, huge and a cantankerous old bugger but he used to make me laugh.

Mum and dad are really quite short and I am the dwarf of the family – a reject, a right short arse little bleeder.

I remember dad flippin' at mum once. It was after she came out of hospital from her hip operation. She was on crutches and she was trying to keep the house clean. We were no help because we were little.

They were rowing because I think mum had found out about Carol. I remember dad grabbing the crutches off her and throwing them into the front garden. Mum fell on the floor and I was trying to lift her up while Darryl went to fetch the crutches for her. It was awful.

Dad even used to take me to see one of his girlfriends at her house. She had a daughter who was about two years old so they used to leave me to watch her. This went on for years. Other people knew it was going on. Me and Darryl knew it was going on.

It must have been really hard on mum because her life could have been so different.

She was actually a really good opera singer and pianist.

Before she met my dad, when she was about 14 or 15 Gang Gang would take her to posh hotels such as the Ritz in London where they would have tea, then she would play the piano for guests in the reception area. Guests would stand and watch her play.

I went to Standhill Infants. After school I would go to my Gang Gang and Mammar Ginny's at Prospect Road for a packet of Snaps and a bag of Mintos.

I loved Mammar and Gang Gang's house because it was always full of nick-nacks and it had furry wallpaper (known today as flock wallpaper). And Mammer used to shout at me when I ran my fingers around the pattern. It was silver and red and embossed. Gang Gang had a clock that chimed. I loved Mammar's ornaments. She would shout at me if I picked them up because she had just polished them and I would get dirty, grubby finger marks on them. She had a silver aeroplane which was an ash tray.

You would put cigarettes in one compartment, matches in another and a lighter in the other.

"That is dirty. Don't touch that!" she'd say.

Mammar Ginny had fiery red hair. She was always fully decked up with her make-up on. She would not go anywhere unless she was made-up. She wore bright red lipstick and bright red nail varnish. Even in her 80s there was not a hair out of place.

Although Gang Gang was huge she was only 4ft 10in. They were like Little and Large. They had a really old-fashioned kind of love and Gang Gang doted on her.

At Christmas they would always come to us for dinner and we would go to theirs for tea. Mammar couldn't cook, she was bloody awful at it, so Gang Gang did it all. But at Christmas Mammar was chuffed to be making her famous sherry trifle with little silver balls and glace cherries on.

Gang Gang smoked cigars at Christmas, but he would smoke a pipe all year round to annoy Mammar because it used to smell. But I used to love the smell of my grandad's pipe and would sit with it in my mouth, pretending to smoke it, till he grabbed it out of me gob.

I remember their silver Christmas tree that was like a big silver pipe cleaner covered in tinsel with huge red glass baubles and multi coloured lights on it. Grandad had a big fairy which he used to let me put on the top of the tree.

We would watch the Morecambe and Wise Christmas Special and eat Mammar's trifle.

They had a caravan at Richmond Park, Skegness, and we would go there for our holidays. The caravan seemed huge to me, but looking back it was probably really small, perhaps a four berth with eight people in it.

Dad drove a dark brown Allegro, then had a bright blue Cortina as well – like a Starsky and Hutch car.

Once, coming back from Skegness in the Allegro we had a massive car crash. This was in the days when you didn't have to wear seat belts. I remember it was raining and a car pulled out in front of us. Dad swerved and went down a verge. Mam was in the front of the car and me and Darryl were in the back.

At the time mum had jet black, long hair, which passed her bum. Just before the car crashed Darryl grabbed mum by her hair and quickly wrapped it round his hand and pulled her backwards. Don't know how he knew to do it before the car hit us, but he did, it must be our Romany blood. He was only about 12 or 13 at the time. If he hadn't done that I'm sure mum would have been killed. The crash was horrible and the car was written off.

I used to feel dead posh when we were in dad's Starsky and Hutch Cortina. I loved watching dad working on cars, taking the wheels off and tinkering under the bonnet.

I never knew my dad's dad as he had died.

The only memories I have of dad's mum, Grandma Flo, was she was a big lady, very bonny, a bit nutty – and she had a hairy mole. She lived in Carrington. We didn't see her often, though she visited us sometimes on a Sunday and would eat dinner with her knife, even the gravy. It used to make mum feel sick. I don't think mum really liked her that much.

When she was in hospital I once went with mum and dad to see her. Grandma Flo told me she had lost her false teeth and told me to go and find them. It was supposed to be a joke. She hadn't lost them at all. I was running up and down the corridors looking for her teeth when I ran into a nurse who was carrying boiling water.

I was still only little, at infants school, at the time.

The water went all over my shoulders and scalded me. I ended up having to be treated at the hospital.

I used to love my dollies when I was little. I had Cheekaboos – Hoppy Boos and Kitty Boos. We couldn't afford Barbie so I had Cindy.

I would play with my Cheekaboos for hours. I always used to make them speak and I would give them voices. They all had their own different voice. I used to make all their clothes and tuck them up in bed every night. We couldn't afford to buy a proper toy caravan for them to sleep in, so I used cardboard boxes to make them one.

I had measles once, so dad bought me Ballerina Cindy with dark hair, but I wanted blonde Cindy. (Only poor people had Cindys, richer kids had Barbies). LOL.

I asked dad if I could have a Barbie instead, so he just chucked it at me and said I was ungrateful.

Overall I didn't have a bad childhood. It was just different to others – better than most, worse than some.

Dad was not a bad person. I wouldn't want to change him really.

Mum would say I was 'spoilt rotten'. I know they would buy me bits and bobs – but I would sooner have had fusses and cuddles and to be told they loved me and were proud of me rather than be bought gifts when I was little. I never felt their love. But I suppose they were parents who never felt comfortable telling their kids they loved them. They were not parents who would say 'I love you'.

Some people show their affections, some don't. They were busy; they had their own lives, always working. Dad was always preoccupied; mum was trying to do her best for me and my brother, but she was so unhappy. She was 45, had two kids – and in the '70s you just did not divorce. You stuck by your man. They met when she was 20. Mum had gone through loads of miscarriages and had gone through hell and high water to make this marriage work. It was not mum's fault. It was not dad's fault.

Nowadays they'd just say: "That's it. We are done. It's over."

In infants school I was bullied because we didn't have much money. We were 'the pit house kids' or 'tramps'. By junior school I was bullied because of the way I looked.

By the time I was eight or nine my blonde hair had turned dark. I was bleaching my hair even at the age of nine or ten.

Instead of using our pocket money to buy Victoria Plum rubbers, me and my friend Tammy used ours to buy peroxide from Boots. Tammy was four or five years older than me. She would get the peroxide and I would go to her house and put it on with a toothbrush. On one occasion she managed to do all her hair, but we ran out of peroxide before I finished mine. Then it turned bright orange. My mum and dad went mad and took me to the hairdressers.

This was in the early 80s and highlights had just come out, so I was really excited that I was having some because I knew it would make me look a little bit different.

One of the things I hated when I was growing up was my nose. It was huge, big and bent and I was always ridiculed at school. I was called Gonzo or Concord, Big Nose, Beak Face or Pinocchio.

I went to Porchester Junior. It was such a lovely school to look at and still is today. We had to walk up the 'donkey steps' to school, so-called because in wartime donkeys would be walked up those steps carrying tools, machinery and things for farm workers working in the fields.

I would run away from school because of the way the other kids treated me. I would have chalk rubbers thrown at the back of my head, would be pushed over in the playground, locked in the outside toilet block, no one would sit next to me in class. They would take my books and steal my pencils and pencil case, or snap my pencils in half.

I was also hit by the teacher Mr Randall because I couldn't tell the time. I was only eight years old, and I couldn't understand the half past the hour. Mum and dad didn't teach us. They probably just thought we knew how to tell the time. Mr Randall had a big, brown, bushy beard which sometimes had food in it, he had yellow fingers and used to smell of tobacco. He was always being nasty.

Once I ran away from school and he ran after me, hit me on the back of the head and dragged me back by the hair. I also used to get the slipper and a cane across the hand because I never used to pay much attention.

Louise Bradley was my best friend and my other good friend was Nicola Eyre. They were bullied as well, especially Louise. I really miss them and wish I could get back in touch. It's a shame how you lose contact with people.

There were exceptions to the horrible teachers at junior school. There was a lovely teacher called Mr Atkins, who was a really old man with grey hair. He used to tell me I was good at gym and drawing. I loved gymnastics and I just wanted to fit in, but I was always so conscious of how I looked in me leotard. All the pretty girls used to do gymnastics. But even though I was good, I could never be the best. It took me a long time to learn back flips and I wasn't very good on the floor – but I was good on the vault and beam. I wanted my dad to say he was proud of me for doing gymnastics – but he never did. He was too tied up with other things. Other parents would actually go to the school to watch their kids do gym displays.

Dad would go to parents' evening, but he was always busy, so all he'd say was: "She needs more homework."

We had to do homework or he would really bollock us.

I always remember a male teacher – a big, fat, bald bloke. When it was PE he would make us change in the classrooms rather than the changing rooms and would make the girls take their tops off and the boys take their pants off. Sometimes he would make us strip off until we were completely nude. He would draw pictures of willies and ladies' bits on the blackboard. I was just eight years old and he would be drawing pictures of how to have sex. We used to have to stand at the side of his desk or sit on his knee. We would read to him and he would touch your bum or 'down below'. I can always remember him getting the sack. He abused a couple of kids at the school and the parents got to know.

I was also bullied by older kids who thought it was funny to eat my sandwiches or chuck books at me. They would grab my bag off me whichever way I went to school.

I knew that I was really ugly. If I caught sight of my reflection I would shut my eyes because I didn't want this ugly thing looking back at me. I used to hate the sight of myself so much I wouldn't have mirrors in my bedroom when I was little and I would just sit and cry about it.

Now, when I look back to this time, I know this was the start of my body dysmorphia – a hatred of the way I look. Obviously, being young and not having the diagnoses you have nowadays, I didn't know it was an illness.

Even then I would pull my lips to make them bigger or pinch my cheeks to make them fatter. I just didn't want to be me. I was ugly.

I grew up with Benny Hill on the TV – where I saw those beautiful blondes with big boobs like Dolly Parton. That's who I wanted to be – a Benny Hill girl or Dolly Parton, who is my icon. I have recently seen Dolly in concert and it was the most amazing experience of my life. One of the things I want to do before I die is meet her.

When I was a kid, not only were all the girls much prettier than me, everyone was so much better dressed with their nice clothes – and they had nice parents.

I even made up a story that I had a boyfriend who was from the USA who used to send me 'charmed' sweets. No one realised my dad actually bought the sweets from the market. I said his name was Richard – which turned out to be ironic bearing in mind what happened in the future. Still no one liked me, but it was worth a try.

I think mum must have known I was bullied at school and wanted to keep me at home, so she used to keep me off school sometimes when dad was at work. I did want to learn. Even now I love learning things. But I would just spend my days at school crying. I was always too scared to read out loud or put my hand up in class to ask questions. I was slow at reading so everyone would take the piss out of me. In the fourth year juniors I was still on the first year Peter and Jane Ladybird books. All I wanted was to be clever, not to be stupid. I realise, looking back, that I had learning difficulties.

In desperation I tried to make friends by giving the kids stuff. I would steal a box of chocolates from mum's room to give them so they wouldn't shout at me. I'd steal packets of fags to give to the older girls and boys hoping they'd be my friend. But they never were.

Deep down I knew I would never fit in. I was not from a privileged background. And in the end I just accepted that was the way it was.

My dream was to be a vet when I grew up but I wasn't clever enough. So I thought when I was older I would like to look after animals, be a show jumper or an actress. All I ever wanted when I was little was to own my own horse.

I wrote to Jim'll Fix It asking if me and Darryl could go on the rides at Blackpool.

I entered competitions. PGL Holidays used to be on TV telling you to fill in a competition form to win a pony. I got the form from Woolworths in Victoria Centre. But I never heard back from any of the competitions. Typical.

From being a really tiny little girl, my pets and my close friends have always been my salvation.

At least I had those. At least I could sit and talk to my rabbits, gerbils, hamsters and budgies. When I had Snowy, my first rabbit, me and dad made the hutch together out of old planks of wood, carpet and chicken wire.

When dad bought me Snowy he was told it and was not going to grow very big. But he grew bigger and bigger. Snowy ended up about two stones so we had to make him a bigger hutch. He was in fact a New Zealand White. He used to do tricks like a dog. Snowy would open his hutch door and follow me around the garden. I would take him into the house and he would sit on the pouffe. When he had enough of being in the house he would thump his back legs, hop back to his hutch and pull the door shut behind him!

Dad had a huge vegetable patch in the garden where he grew sprouts, potatoes and cabbages. Snowy used to love eating the cabbages. I even used to keep the caterpillars off the vegetables in my bedroom.

My next door neighbour's daughter had rabbits and she wanted to breed them because she wanted more. The first litter were born dead, but in the next litter two survived, Speedy and Hoppy. I kept Speedy and Hoppy and also had my neighbour's rabbit Bungie.

I would feed my bunnies every morning before going to school. One morning, when I was 11 (I had just started Frank Wheldon Comprehensive school) I looked out of the window and saw Snowy lying in the garden. By then I had had him for six years. It was a really cold and frosty November morning.

"What's Snowy doing?" I thought.

And his cage door was open. I knew Snowy would not normally come out in the cold.

I went out and found Snowy slumped over a brick. The other three rabbits were strewn across the bottom of our allotment.

Dad found out our next door neighbour had killed Snowy – and all of the others. His two daughters had four rabbits and he couldn't afford to keep them so he necked them. But he needed a viable story so he killed ours as well to make it look as if someone else had killed his kids' rabbits.

He made the mistake of boasting about it to someone – so dad punched him. One of the neighbours heard them fighting and came to see what was going on. He told my dad he and his wife had heard Snowy screaming in the night and looked out of the window to see what was happening. They saw the man in our garden. The evil bastard.

Losing my rabbits really messed me up. It absolutely devastated me. I was 11 years old and my best friend in the world had been killed for no reason.

My pets were more than just animals. Snowy was everything to me.

Even today I can't communicate with people properly, but I feel more like an animal person. I find it quite difficult to communicate with people, but with animals I suppose I just feel at peace. I feel secure around them, but I don't feel secure around humans, strange as that may sound to some of you.

It seemed as if my childhood was done, so by the age of 11 I already thought I was an adult.

# The Worry of Being a Parent

For those of you who don't know I'm a single mum with a little boy 'H' (Henri) who is now 12 going on 40.

God, this boy is far too knowledgeable for his own good. Think he gets his brains from me (er – not).

But he wasn't always so outgoing and confident as he is today.

You see when he was at baby school, sorry junior school, he was severely bullied.

And even though it was for a short while, my God it took its toll on him.

Because I was a working mum unfortunately I couldn't afford to be a stay-at-home mum. And with his dad leaving us, I didn't want to go on benefits. So I did have to work – which made me feel like crap I'll tell you.

So H had to stay in school for his dinners. Day after day I would pack his Barney bear sandwiches, packet of Wotsits and his yoghurt – which would have kept me going all week.

But he came home some days starving hungry.

"H baby you can't be hungry angel," I'd say.

"I am mummy. Can I have my tea now please?"

And this was only an hour or so after his lunch at school.

Now I know kids are pigs and they eat you out of house and home, but H was never ever a big eater.

At weekends he never ate much at all, which made me question his eating regime.

Then he started being really withdrawn, not his usual bubbly talkative self. he had gone from being this motormouth six-year old wanting to know everything about everything to a withdrawn, frightened little boy.

'Oh my God, it's me. He is turning into what I was like', I thought. And I wasn't going to let this happen, not to my baby.

'My boy is not going to go through this'.

"Baby, come and talk to mummy," I said. "What's wrong angel? Just tell me. It doesn't matter what it is. I'm your mummy, you're not in trouble."

Well, I wasn't expecting the reaction I got.

He was only six and he sobbed and sobbed in my arms for hours.

"I don't eat my sandwiches."

"Why?"

"They take my lunch box and squash them and throw my crisps away."

"OK baby, who does?"

"The big boys."

Well, that was it.

You will know if you are a parent the anger you feel if your child is hurt or upset.

The next morning I kept him off school and went to see his headteacher – for what good that did. All he said was: "Oh no, Miss Walker. We don't have bullying at our school."

So I had a word with his class teacher and asked her to keep an eye on him at play times as this was when the bullying was happening to him. To make things easier for him I decided to let him stay for school dinners.

He still wasn't himself, but at least I knew he would be eating.

I had a friend (well, I say 'friend') who I paid to look after H after school for an hour until I came home from work. I didn't mind paying her. I paid her basically to give him some dinner. Oh what a mistake that one was. She never did give him any dinner. Oh well, you live and learn don't you?

Anyway, I got to hers one day and H came running down the stairs to me.

"Fucking hell. What's happened to you?"

He had a huge black eye, a massive lump on his head and his body was covered in bruises. I was in complete shock.

This so-called mate of mind didn't even bother ringing me at work to tell me what had happened to my son.

I just picked him up an looked at this vile woman who I had trusted with my little boy and left. I couldn't even speak to her, not even to tell her to go fuck herself.

He cried all the way home.

"Mummy, please don't make me go to school again," he said.

"Baby. You will never go back to that school ever."

He told me that at dinner break (and the school didn't even ring me), that four older boys made him stand behind the bushes then just hit and kicked him on the floor.

The teacher did nothing to these kids.

So I went back to the school again to have it out with the head, in the mother of all moods.

All I got was: "Oh we are really sorry for what happened."

"Are you taking the piss?" I said. "Sorry? What good is that?"

H never went back there. After that, I found him the most amazing school – which was, in fact, my junior school.

If you are a parent reading this book, just listen to your kids. Don't judge them. Don't cast aspersions. Just listen to them.

Talk to them as little adults, not as children. They need to learn how to speak with you and you have got to be an honest parent.

When I look back at the people who bullied me I never feel sorry for them. People say you should feel sorry for a bully, but bullies know what they are doing. Why should you feel sorry for them? They know if they make someone cry. They know it is wrong and they are hurting another person. So why should you feel sorry for someone who is fully aware that what they are doing is wrong? You should give the victim your sympathy.

The bullies need to stop.

But it's down to the parents. They need to bring their children up with respect for others so they won't bully.

There's no respect nowadays and it's getting worse, with gangs involved. We had gangs years ago, but they are even more notorious now, carrying knives and guns.

Kids of eight and ten are smashing up property. The world is evolving, but family values have changed so much to even ten years ago. If we had done anything remotely like children are doing now we would have been petrified of the police, our parents and the teachers, because we did have respect.

I think nowadays, unfortunately some parents don't have any respect for authority, so how can they expect their children to have any? It's a shame that some of these parents think it is acceptable for their child to go through life hurting other children.

Parents need to drill into kids – you have respect for authority and you can't go through life hurting people. It's for the parent to nip it in the bud, and if they don't it's their fault. They know if they've got a naughty kiddie or not, so they really need to keep an eye on that child's behaviour – and they should think of the poor kid who's being bullied. It's not hard to look after your child. You have children to love and nurture them. At the end of the day you are the parent and a child needs guidance. It is up to mums and dads to guide their children towards being better adults.

I was bullied for a number of reasons and the bullies got away with it. I never did stick up for myself until I was older.

Kids do not need to be scared to tell someone that they are being bullied. It has to stop. Even though kids are frightened to tell parents and teachers that they are being bullied, it is easier to tell someone and let them know that you are being bullied, than to go through the pain and hurt the bully is putting you through.

Bullies will have to face the rest of their life knowing what they have done to those people they bullied.

To those who are being a bully now – that torment will be

handed out to you later because of Karma.

If you are reading this, and you are abusing another person physically or mentally, then you should stop and ask yourself, why?

Do you really want to live the rest of your life questioning what you have done to another human being? Is it really worth that?

So you had better always be nice to people and never shit on them.

Everyone is a human, an individual and life is too short, far too short, to be nasty and hateful to people.

# Staggering Through Comp

I was absolutely shitting myself.

It was September 1981. Jesus Christ Almighty I was starting comprehensive school. For years I had wanted to be a teenager – now I really didn't want to be.

Just before the summer holidays our teachers at our junior school took us to Frank Wheldon Comprehensive for a day visit.

I always remember all the kids being huge and really tall. I was so petrified. I was only 11 – and such a little short arse, so everyone seemed so tall to me.

At the Comp they had a 'house system' named after forests in Nottinghamshire. I was placed in Sherwood. I only had a couple of friends, and to make matters worse, they were placed in Thorsby house. I was not a very sociable kid, not very good at making friends. I didn't know how to interact, how to talk to people.

I went with my mum to buy my uniform. I was going mad because I didn't want to wear the black and green tie, but she made me wear it. On the first day mum made me go to my neighbour Betty Wheatley to show her how grown up I looked and Betty just laughed at me.

Then came the moment I had to do the walk of death to school. I can not even put it into words how scared I was.

Put it this way – if they had invented Tenna Ladies 27 years ago I would have got through a couple of boxes on that morning walk to school.

I was lucky enough to have three very good friends, three sisters who lived across the road (more beautiful than me of course), who I loved very dearly. But two of them were older than me, so they were not in the same year at school.

They were like my sisters. There was Sandra (gorgeous with great big boobs); Theresa, my 'bestest friend' in the world; and Amanda, a year younger than me, with her beautiful fiery red hair. Their mum and dad were the Simpsons. Their mum was called Lilly, dad was Alan Simpson. My other friends on my road were Tammy and Stewart. We all walked together on that first day.

I arrived at school not knowing anyone. I was absolutely petrified. I stood there like a lost sheep, clutching on to my school bag and my sandwich box. We were made to stand in the quad, a huge area where first years were assembled before teachers came to get them. The quad was where you could go and play.

I remember looking round and thinking why was no one speaking to me? But I suppose I was to blame, because I was not speaking to anyone as I was so frightened. When we got to our first tutor group our tutor make us sit quite close to each other, so I made friends there and then.

For once, I was actually quite lucky and made friends really quickly and was not bullied by anyone my age other than a couple of girls who were quite bitchy and called me a slag and a tramp. But it was the older kids at Frank Wheldon who really made my life a misery.

The headteacher was Mrs Purdu, called 'The Dragon' at school because she was very strict and hard. She didn't like my brother Darryl, but she was really nice to me. She hated him because he was a right 'bogga'.

When I was 13 or 14 we had a lovely German teacher, Miss Panayiotou, who told us she was George Michael's sister! I always remember her wearing loads of make-up and having very dark olive skin. She had huge backcombed black hair. I loved French and German, and did particularly well at German.

Miss Panayiotou asked me back to her house as I was struggling with homework and she knew I really enjoyed German. I remember her saying: "If you come round, I have my brother staying with me. You might know who he is. He's got a song in the charts. His band is called Wham!"

"Yes, of course it is," I thought.

Me being a stroppy fucking teenager, with the conversation of a slug, I didn't end up going. What a tit I was!

A couple of weeks later Miss Panayiotou came into school to say she was leaving. She was going on tour with her brother, she announced, to be George Michael's make-up artist.

No one believed her at school, then it came out in the papers that it was true. She was George Michael's sister.

I could have met George Michael. If I could have changed anything in my childhood it would have been that I had gone that night.

Can you imagine – me meeting George Michael?! Ay up – you never know if I had met him a couple of years later down the line I might've been able to turn him straight. I should have been so lucky.

I suppose I had my first boyfriend when I was about 11 or 12. He was 14. And he was the reason I started to get bullied so severely. The girlfriend he had broken up with was 14 as well and she and her friend used to kick the shit out of me because they knew we were kissing and stuff. Her friend used to call me a slag and beat the living crap out of me, on one occasion breaking my nose.

About six or seven of them, including these two, used to target me when I was on my own, and would even threaten my friends so they would leave me.

"You stay away from him, he's my boyfriend," his ex would say. She was really vile to me. She would spit in my face and chuck glue on me. We had pots of glue at school, and once when I was going to the toilet two girls held me while she poured glue in my hair.

Once when I was walking past Sherwood block where there is a really high bridge nearby. They pushed me into the bridge and tried to push me over it. The bridge is over buildings and the drop is about 25ft, so high we used to go parascending over it, that's how tall it was. Christ, looking back, they could have killed me really.

While I was at Frank Wheldon we had school roller discos at Carlton Forum, a leisure complex. I loved roller skating and would like to have gone more often, but I was always too frightened because the older girls were there with their boyfriends.

Once I went there with a friend and she had to leave early, so I left the Forum intending to skate home on my own.

But a group of them were waiting for me outside and I got the usual treatment. I remember thinking to myself 'don't cry', but they were hurting me so much.

When I got home mum and dad were out. They used to go to Gedling Miners Welfare Club, and Darryl was 16 then so he was out with his mates.

So I just went to bed and cried feeling sorry for myself, cuddling my cat Clara.

There was a clique at school which I always wanted to be in, but I never was.

I suppose this is the reason why I'm not good around everyday people. I am different. I look different. I have different outlook on life to most people I should imagine. So I find it easier to talk to and communicate with people who are different, like me. Even today I am still wary and don't trust 'normal' people, whatever normal people are. I always find they have deep-set issues and are so quick to judge. I am just waiting for them to say or do something nasty. My friends nowadays are different to the norm – which, thank God, I am glad of. I would not want bog standard friends. I like creative souls; I like different people with varied views. I enjoy the company and conversation of creative souls. I'm not bothered if they live different lives to 'Mr and Mrs Smith' with two point four children living in suburbia. That's why I love the people I love.

I was with my boyfriend at the Comp for about three or four years. But throughout that time I was sick and tired of being bullied.

One day I was beaten up by a girl because she thought I was trying to steal her boyfriend Michael, who was in my class. I wasn't. I just used to talk to him because he wasn't very clever like me, so he was in the same remedial classes as me. We were really good friends, but she did not believe that.

I remember once going to a school disco. Superman by Black Lace, was playing as I walked to the doors (now that did scar me for life).

She grabbed me, pulled me down and head butted me at the bottom of the stairs. This girl was one you did not mess about with.

Often when I was beaten up I would just go home and say I had been in a fight at school. It was just one of those things. I wouldn't say much more because I didn't want my parents to be embarrassed, because I wasn't a tough nut like them and my brothers. Kids were always fighting, so you thought nothing of going home with a black eye. We were not wrapped up in cotton wool. These were the days when you would have a smack off your mum and dad or a caning from the teacher.

In a strange way I used to really admire this girl who was head-butting me because she was so hard. She came from such a hard family of nutters that people had respect for her. But I was not like that; I was quite quiet.

But this head-butting incident was to be the turning point.

I had had enough.

I remember sitting at home with my cat Clara thinking 'I am not ever going to be like this again. I am not going to let anyone hit me again'.

So I changed. I wasn't a bully, but I was a little shit. I would say nasty things. If someone said something nasty to me I would give it back tenfold and make them cry.

And I stopped going to school.

It still hurts today that my best friend from Frank Wheldon Comp Joanna Gibbs sold stories about me which were complete and utter bullshit when I came out of the Big Brother house.

I loved her. She was my best friend, like my sister. Our family took her to Spain where we had an apartment. When I came out of the 'house', I found out all my so-called friends that I had in Nottingham had sold me out. While I was in the Big Brother house how were my family to know whether the things they were reading were the truth?

I read one story where she had given them a photo of me and told the papers I was shagging when I was 13 years old. If anyone was shagging it was her, not me at all. Everything she said was complete and utter shit. She sold a bullshit story and I hope she is having a miserable, shit existence of a life, the rotten cow. You can't do that to people. She did not give two shits about my mum or my son reading that. I lost touch with her when I was about 20 years old and I was not in Big Brother until I was 35. She did it for greed, the greedy pig. I loved her so much – and I used to love seeing her mum Maggie. You can't sell your mates out.

Even my friends who I had for ten years sold their stories for money, fucking money hungry people. How can they do that to a friend?

I wasn't having sex with my first boyfriend. It was just 'trying bits and bobs', a kiss and a fumble, not proper shagging.

But I was drinking.

When I was 12 I went to Louise Cooke's party. Me and my boyfriend drank so much Thunderbird we had to be taken to hospital to have our stomachs pumped. My boyfriend was actually in a coma.

On one occasion me and my boyfriend were sitting down Valley Road listening to music. My mum had bought me a big Toshiba twin tape with two huge speakers. Me and my ex were sitting in the grounds listening to our 'boom box' when a group of lads came by and stole my stereo. One of the lads punched me and I ran off. Then they started beating my boyfriend up. He was getting the shit kicked out of him until Darryl came down with a group of his mates and the gang ran off.

Often on a Sunday afternoon at home we would play three card brag in the kitchen after tea. It was some time after this incident that we were sitting playing cards and we looked out of the window and saw some lads in the park. I told our Darryl: "That's the lads who beat up my boyfriend and smacked me."

Darryl ran out of the kitchen into the garden and leapt over the fence at the bottom, even though there was a ten to twelve foot drop. He ran across a neighbour's garden to get over the road and into the field where he head-butted one of the lads. My brother used to love fighting. He was a nutter.

The lad's nose just split and it ending up with everyone fighting on the Rec and the police were called. Darryl was arrested and got done for GBH.

But it wasn't them. It wasn't the right gang! So it was me who got our Darryl into trouble.

So here we are in the 1980s and the trouble just goes on and on.

My boyfriend used to work at Carlton Golf Range collecting golf balls, so I often used to meet him there. One day I went to meet him but he wasn't there, so I walked back to his house on my own. I was 12 or 13 at the time, wearing my school uniform. It was about 7.30–8am. I noticed a man walking nearby, and every time I moved he followed me. It was quite open, but he was at the side of a hedgerow. I wondered what he was doing, but didn't think anything was going to happen. But I was really scared when he grabbed me. That close up I could tell he was filthy with potholed skin and blackheads, scruffy and vile. He pushed me into the hedge and ripped my tights trying to lift my skirt up. He got me on the floor and touched me down below. I was so scared I could not even scream or move. It all happened so quickly and I knew what was happening was wrong, but I was quite naïve.

Luckily when a bloke came walking by with a dog he ran off. The bloke asked if I was OK, then I went to my boyfriend's and told him what had happened. He came down to the fields with his brother to look for him, but they couldn't find him.

We went to the police station and the school was notified so everyone found out. I was horrified when I found that out. It turned out this man had raped three or four girls from our area, so I was so lucky, God forbid, that did not happen to me – I was so lucky that other bloke turned up.

Is it any wonder this completely messed me up with men? I still have an apprehension with straight men and don't feel really comfortable round them. With gay men I'm fine, because I know there is nothing sexual and they are not going to try and take advantage. With my experience of straight men there's always an ulterior motive. Gay men want a friendship from you.

But I guess the straight men I have met did not want to be friends. They always wanted a sexual relationship, which I never wanted, pushing to get you into bed.

Looking back, I think my problems with men stem from that incident: it was that bastard's fault. He took a part of me away that I will never get back. I could never have a friendship with a straight man without wondering 'is this leading to sex'? And 'if it's never going to happen is he going to be violent'?

When I was about 16 I thought I was in love with my boyfriend and had sex with him for the first time. But I didn't enjoy it at all. I just felt it was wrong and I didn't want to do it.

Before I leave my schooldays there are some people I would like to mention from Frank Wheldon Comp – friends who played a big part in my life. I had such a good time with Emma Hall, a German girl, with lovely long, blonde, natural hair.

I want to mention my drama teacher Miss Lewis who taught me

I could pretend to be someone else. And she always encouraged me. She would say 'you are good at this' or 'you are brilliant that'. For the first time someone encouraged me and was really proud of me. I loved drama. I hated my appearance so much I could pretend not to be me! I realised then that I wanted to be an actress. And I still have that same feeling today: I'm happier being in someone else's role. Even in Big Brother it wasn't really me – but more about that later.

I got a grade A 'o' level in drama and failed everything else.

In my schooldays rock music was also very important to me. I loved Guns 'n' Roses and Black Sabbath and would get wasted in Victoria Centre flats when I was 15 years old. With my backcombed hair and tight dresses I used to go to Easy Street, Central Park, Ritz's, Rock City and the Cross Keys pub. I would go to Rock City with older people, wearing so much make-up I could pretend to be someone else. I used to cake it on – bright blue eye shadow – I used to put that much on, it used to make my eyelids heavy and when I blinked the make-up would crease. I wore white lipstick, had an orange face and bright pink cheeks. Once I tried to look like Whitney Houston, wearing eye shadow in stripes. Good God, I must have looked such a twat.

I would get drunk then stay at my friend's. (She was always drunk too, so drunk she wouldn't notice how much I had had).

The good old days of the '80s. It was when I was 15 or 16 that I first met the man who was to play the biggest part in my life to date. I met him at Central Park where he was playing lead guitar in a local rock band. He also sang. But more about him later...

In the world of rock music I never felt threatened. This was one of the only times I felt comfortable, being around rockers and rock chicks – perhaps because they were not the norm. They didn't have any inhibitions; they just wanted to enjoy themselves.

It was a brilliant era and I am so lucky that I experienced that first hand. There was no bitchiness, just a fun good time – and the music. I also loved Motley Crue, T Rex, Def Leppard – they were just the best years ever.

Looking back I wish I had gone to school more. I knew I was thick and I could never spell, but I did want to learn. I used to pretend to go to school, but I would go to town instead, or sit at Carlton Precinct, or go back to my house because my parents would be out. They never knew I wasn't at school. They would have gone nuts. When I was 15 years old I was probably going to school about one day a week dreaming of the time I could leave and become an actress.

Then it was my 16th birthday and I was about to suffer a terrible loss.

My Gang Gang was still a massive figure in my life. And Gang Gang was a massive guy, a giant. My grandad to me was my life; I loved him wholeheartedly. As a little girl I used to love sitting in his big silver car which had cushions and nodding dogs in the back. He had a caravan in Skegness and he would take me on the boating lake. He was strict – but I knew he loved me. He used to pick me up and put me on his knee. I loved going round to his house and sitting with him while he had his cigars and pipe. I loved that smell – because it was my grandad, with his Mintos and his cheese snaps. I used to sit in the garden and watch him polish his car. I was always excited as a little girl going to see Gang Gang because he made me happy.

When Gang Gang was in his 70s he became ill. He couldn't get out of bed and was just not himself and we didn't know why at first.

It turned out he had incurable lung and renal cancer.

He was admitted to City Hospital in Nottingham and I went to see him in a hospice.

Gang Gang used to weigh about 18 stones, built like a brick shithouse, ever so handsome with white hair and beautiful eyes.

Now he looked like a skeleton, all skin and bone with green and yellow skin. He weighed about seven stones. We wanted him to come home so he wouldn't die in a hospice.

It hurt my heart. I cannot even put it into words. He was dying in front of us and I could not do anything; no one could stop it – this person who I loved and who was not going to be there anymore.

God is quite horrible in that respect. If God is good why take away people who love you and people you love?

Gang Gang never did anyone any wrong; he was always loving and caring. He never did anything to anyone. Why give him, someone with such a pure heart, cancer?

He had never been ill until now.

He came home and my dad Cliff would go round to look after him. Gang Gang was so weak he could not get up the stairs so we brought his bed into the front room.

The stress of Gang Gang's illness made Mamma ill as well.

One day after school he seemed better so I went round with a bag of Mintos. There was just me, Mamma and grandad.

We sat watching their black and white telly and Mamma made us salmon and cucumber sandwiches.

I remember Gang Gang smelled funny – he smelt ill. His skin was different and his eyes were dull; they had lost that sparkle. Mamma sat in a chair and I sat on the bed with grandad.

Despite his appearance he seemed a little better in himself. I went home and said to mum: "I think grandad is getting better."

And he was alright for a couple of days before my 16th birthday.

Then on the morning of my birthday at 4am Cliff rang. Darryl answered the phone then came to wake me up.

"We've got to go to Mamma and Gang Gang's," he said.

My brothers Kevin and Robert and their wives were there.

I went into the front room and sat on Gang Gang's bed with him. He held my hand and told me he loved me and sang happy birthday. He shut his eyes and went to Jesus. And as soon as he shut his eyes a tear trickled down his cheek. I thought he had just gone to sleep. But Robert came into the room and within a split second he knew Gang Gang had died.

No one said anything. Mamma just fell on the floor and could not stop crying. He had gone.

Gang Gang's death crushed my dad. It was the first time I had seen him cry. Cliff thought the world of my grandad.

But it was after Gang Gang's death that mum moved in with Mamma – when Cliff cheated on her and she could not stand any more. My life has been difficult, but my mum has been through a hell of a lot too; her life should be made into a film.

When mum moved in with Mamma she had to buy all kinds of things for the house which was cold with old, rotting windows and no central heating. She bought a washing machine and gas heaters to make it more comfortable. She had moved out, but she never came to terms with what Cliff had done.

Gang Gang fought for his country and was in concentration camps. He always worked. He always did stuff for people, always putting others before himself.

He died on my 16th birthday and was buried on Darryl's 21st birthday.

When Gang Gang died 90 per cent of me died with him. I loved my grandad. I think he gave me the love I always felt I needed from my dad. I got that love from grandad and my Aunty Ivy.

I felt different as a person when I was with my grandad. Without him my heart used to be really heavy; as if it was black inside. But when I was with him it was not; I felt normal, light.

When Gang Gang died he took my heart with him.

# Aunt Ivy

Before I leave my schooldays completely I really want to talk about my Aunty Ivy as she played such a huge part during my younger years and growing up.

My Aunty Ivy was my mamma's sister, (so I know that doesn't exactly make her my aunty), but she was only a year older than me mum so my mamma brought them up together like sisters.

Our Ivy was married to me Uncle Ernest and they had a daughter Ann.

I have already mentioned earlier in the book just how much I loved Aunty Ivy, and how I loved spending time with her in her HUGE house. (In reality it was just a normal sized house, but I guess when you're a kid everything seems bigger and different – and that's how the house seemed to me.)

My best childhood memories are of times spent with Aunty Ivy. No matter how bad I was feeling, or what I was going through, she tried to make it better – and usually she did.

Weekends (Saturdays and Sunday afternoons after swimming especially) were my happiest days with her. Even though we fell out when I was about eight years old because she drowned some baby mice, I still loved her more than you could ever imagine.

I used to stay at our Ivy's on Saturday nights and we would watch Jim'll Fix It and her favourite programme Tales of the Unexpected. She would make beans on toast and Ovaltine for me. We would sit for hours playing Buckaroo, Jaws or Kaplunk – just me, Aunty Ivy and Cilla, her little Yorkshire terrier.

She would let me go into our Ann's bedroom (which had never been changed from when she was a little girl) where I would play with her dolls and dress Cilla up in the dolls' clothes – just like I did with my cat Mindy.

No matter how poorly she was Aunty Ivy was always loving and caring. She always used to say to me that the best thing in the world – even better than a smile – was to give a big cuddle. I never got them from mum and dad, so it was important to me as she made me feel loved.

Aunty Ivy had suffered a couple of nervous breakdowns years before when Uncle Ernie had a heart attack and died. I can't remember him at all, but mum said it was as though her life ended the day he died.

After Uncle Ernie passed away our Ann lived with Ivy for a few years until she was in her late teens, then she got married. Our Ann was stunning: long black hair, dark skin, beautiful, a bit like Catherine Zeta Jones. When she left, that just left Aunty Ivy alone with Cilla. That little dog was her life and her reason to keep on living. Cilla was like her daughter; she had had her for 18 years and took her everywhere with her.

Sadly, it was while I was still at my senior school that things took a nasty turn for Aunty Ivy.

I was about 14 years old when she started deteriorating at an alarming rate.

Looking back now, as an adult, I realise that the things she was saying and doing meant she was a person in deep depression, in mental breakdown. But as a child I wouldn't know what the hell was happening to her, or what she was going through, would I?

But at 14 I knew something was severely wrong with me poor Aunty Ivy when she did go over the edge.

It was the death of little Cilla that did it – the final straw she did not need. Aunty Ivy had been pushed over the edge now and unfortunately there was no way back.

Aunty Ivy was only in her late 50s when Cilla passed away and she found herself with no one to love or look after. I did used to go round to her house, but not as much as I used to. And I had stopped staying there at weekends. God, I wish more than anything that I had continued to stay with her, then maybe she would still be here today.

Also mum had stopped going round as they'd had a fall out over my dad.

Aunty Ivy's moods started changing. She would shout and be quite nasty. I couldn't understand why, but I know now it was her mental health.

But worst of all, was what she did.

Aunty Ivy would go to the Post Office across the road to collect her pension, give some of it away to whoever was in there – and eat the rest.

I remember mum getting phone calls: "Come and fetch your Ivy. She's at it again."

Luckily mum was very good friends with the postmistress, who would look after Aunty Ivy while mum was on her way to fetch her.

I remember once I was at home watching TV and there was a knock on the door. It was Aunty Ivy. She had walked all the way up Valley Road to our house (which was a long way I'm telling you) – and she was completely naked – no pants, nothing. I remember Aunty Ivy crying uncontrollably in our kitchen, but mum and dad wouldn't let me in. Mum wrapped her up and my dad took her back home. I think mum went and stayed with her that night.

This kind of situation happened a few times, where she would go for a walk and completely forget to put her clothes on, then the police would bring her round to our house.

People around where we lived were so lovely and understanding. They knew my aunty was such a lovely, kind person to everyone she knew. She was the salt of the earth and never did any wrong to anyone.

The last day I saw my aunty before she was sectioned she was going for her daily walk, completely naked again – but this time she was walking a cucumber up the road dragging it behind her on Cilla's old lead. Shortly after the police brought her home to us she was sectioned and taken to Mapperley Hospital.

Now Mapperley Hospital for the mentally ill was an asylum, a really horrid place, a nuthouse with padded cells. It was where one of the Krays was placed in the '60s.

While she was in there mum took me, our Darryl and his friend Rich to see her. I don't think mum realised just how bad it was going to be – or she wouldn't have taken us. I don't think anything could have prepared us for what we saw that day. It was horrific.

I was only 14 and our Darryl was 19 (as was Rich), but it still scared the living crap out of us.

Oh God, the smell – as soon as we walked through the doors it hit us like a ton of bricks. It was a concoction of fag smoke, bleach and pungent wee.

There were patients walking around in their white nightgowns with nothing underneath them. They were the type of gown you do up at the back and there is a split so you could see they had no pants on. Some patients were just sat on cold, concrete floors; others were in chairs. But they all rocked back and forth. The screams along the hospital corridors were awful.

After getting through that part of the hospital we had to walk up at least seven or eight flights of stairs. I remember them: they looked as if they came from a horror film – all rusty cast iron with paint flaking off. When we got to the top there was a stretcher in the corridor with a sheet over it. Our Darryl made me cry because he said there was a dead body under it.

But while he and Rich were laughing at me they got the shit scared out of them – when all of a sudden a bloke shot up from under it with a fag hanging out of his mouth shouting at them: "Giz a shmoke! Giz a shmoke!"

They turned white and ran off screaming toward me and mum! I nearly wet myself as I was laughing so much. That was justice for them scaring me.

But the laughter was about to stop as we walked through double doors, then through a single door – to see this white room where Aunty Ivy sat slumped in a smelly old orange chair.

She was unrecognisable. Within a few weeks, perhaps not even that, she had gone from a healthy, beautiful lady to a grey old skeleton. I'll always remember looking into her eyes when I held her hand. She had lost the will to live – and she was still only in her 60s.

It was too much for our Darryl and Rich so they went for a fag while me and mum stayed with Aunty Ivy. I remember sitting on the end of her bed. Mum was cradling her like a baby and they were both crying. I just sat there not knowing what to do and feeling scared.

Aunty Ivy was in the mental hospital for months, but we never visited again as it was too much to handle for my mum and I was too young to go alone.

When she was released from hospital she had lost her beautiful home and was placed in an OAP bungalow which she hated and where she never really settled.

She seemed to get better after a couple of months so mum and dad decided we would go on holiday to Spain. We didn't take Darryl as he was 19 and didn't want to go with us anyway. In the early '80s mobile phones were not as readily available as they are now and payphones were useless. They never worked, especially at cheap times of night, so it was difficult to ring home. So mum and dad only rang home now and again.

We were into our second week when dad rang home and our Darryl gave him the worse news imaginable.

My Aunty Ivy had gone. She had passed away and we were not there.

My Aunty Ivy, the lady who truly loved me, had been taken away from me for good. She would never cuddle me again, never tell me things will work out for the best in the end.

I remember watching my mum and dad when they were on the phone. Mum's face just dropped and she started crying and my dad just held her. I wasn't at the phone box with them. I was at the pool, but I could see.

I thought something had happened to our Darryl. The first thing that came into my head was: 'oh he's been arrested again', or 'he had had a party and the house had been smashed up'.

When mum and dad came over to me my dad just said: "Our Ivy is gone. She's gone to Jesus now."

I felt as if my heart had been ripped out of my chest. I had never felt pain like this before in my life. Unfortunately, it was not the last time my heart would be ripped to bits. Our Darryl told dad that the funeral was a couple of days later.

Dad tried to get a flight back but we couldn't get one – so I couldn't even say goodbye and thank you for loving me.

To this day we still do not know where she is buried. The cemetery staff lost the burial plans and our Darryl can't bloody remember either. Also, we never knew just how she did pass away as it was never mentioned.

But looking back, her death was a Godsend for her as she could finally be back with my Uncle Ernest and Cilla, her beloved little Yorkie terrier.

Aunty Ivy gave me so much happiness when I needed to feel loved and secure or just needed a great big hug. She was always there. I just hope she didn't pass away on her own and that someone was holding her when she did go to Jesus that day.

So Aunty Ivy: thank you for teaching me not to give a tiny rat's ass what anyone ever thinks of me. I loved you then and love you now – and will love you for the rest of my life.

# The Pain of Being Fat

I wanted to stay on at school to do acting in the sixth form or to go to drama college.

This caused a real argument with my dad who told me: "If you're living under my roof you have to work and pay board."

So he got me a job as a cutter at Speedo, which made swimming costumes and trunks at Emery's Road, Gedling, Notts. But I couldn't do it because I was left handed, so they gave me a job on a machine as an overlocker which I did for about six months.

Gone were my dreams of being on the silver screen.

And by this time I was so sick and tired of people taking the piss out of me because I was skinny that I actually put on weight. I was really short, but I weighed about 11½ stones.

From the very first day when I walked into Speedo I hated it: from the smell and the bosses to the job and some of the people. But there was nothing I could do about it. I knew I had to work or I would have nowhere to live.

Then I applied for a job as a packer which was on a different site at Ascot Road, Bobbers Mill in Aspley where the people were really lovely. It was a small place with only 12 people, a real tight knit factory. The women were lovely so I was really happy. But Speedo started to expand – so they moved the machinists from Emery's Road to us at Bobbers Mill. Now there were about 100–150 of us and the bitchiness was terrible. It was the most awful time – and because of my size I started to be severely bullied all over again, by a couple of machinists in particular. I was big, about 14 stones by now. I was this big teenager with massive, fat arms, fat arse, the most horrendous legs – and no boobs. I had bigger tits in the rolls of fat on my fat back than on my front. I never used to wear a bra because my boobs were too small. I was too fat, but my boobs were too small! The women thought it was funny to shout really vile names across the canteen so people would look and laugh at me.

I used to think 'I do not want to be here anymore'.

When I was 16 I met a lad who was shorter than me and as I used to wear high heels, I was always quite a bit taller than him. In contrast to me he was really skinny. You could actually see his ribs and he had knobbly knees. He lived with his mum and dad.

I'm not including any of my ex's names because I don't want to give them any notoriety, but they all know who they are and what they did to me. I don't want to give them any satisfaction knowing their names are in this book. So I'll just call this one 'Mr Green'.

I was still working at Speedo, earning about £100 a week on piece rate (which in those days was a hell of a lot of money) and Mr Green made me give him all my wages. He would take my wages off me on a Friday, leaving me with just my board to give my mum. It was a power thing for him: financially, emotionally and mentally controlling me.

I bought him his first car, a Mark II Escort.

And he was the start of my violent relationships.

He knew I had no self respect and he knew I hated myself. I would cry because I was fat. I couldn't be naked around him because I was ashamed how ugly I was. I guess it didn't help with him calling me fat and ugly day after day, drilling it into me – so I started eating even more, getting fatter and fatter and fatter. He could eat as much as he liked and still be really skinny. But even now if I ate like a normal person I would quickly pile on the pounds and be obese because when I eat, I EAT. It is scary how much I can eat – and I won't stop until I am actually sick. I have never had a healthy relationship with food. I can go days and it doesn't faze me if I don't eat.

One day we had a massive argument at his parents' house over money and I could see it in his eyes – he really wanted to hurt me. It was at a point in our relationship when he was taking money off me and I was trying to stick up for myself. He asked for my wages and I said no – the first time I had said no to him. I wanted to keep my money; I wanted things for myself. I was 16 or 17, not buying clothes, make-up or perfume. I wanted stuff for me.

His face was like thunder and his whole character changed.

It went from: 'where's your wages?' to 'give me your wages' and he grabbed them off me.

There was a plate glass door in the front room and as I tried to get out he pushed my head towards it with such force I'm sure he wanted it to go through the door. I put my hands and arms out trying to protect my face. Because of the force with which he pushed me and because of my weight, my hands went right through the thick glass breaking my thumb.

But even worse, my thumb was just hanging by a piece of skin and there was glass sticking up from the vein – this huge great big fuck off bit of glass stuck up from my wrist with the vein popped up and glass gone through it. I remember screaming because I was so frightened.

At first I was sitting on the floor not realising what had happened and I couldn't understand where the pool of blood kept coming from.

My thumb was just flopping. It was unbelievable, the most horrific thing I have ever seen. I still remember the smell, the stench of the blood – yet there was no pain at all. I was trying to pull the glass out, but the more I pulled it the blood was like a fountain.

I went to the bathroom and got a towel to wrap round my hand – but he didn't give a shit. I could have been bleeding to death.

I wrapped the towel round my hand – and he went fucking nuts because I got blood on it. He kept shouting 'stupid bitch' at me. He didn't give a flying fuck. He was on the phone to a glazier!

All he could say was: "What's mum and dad going to say about the door and the mess?!"

He took me to hospital eventually and I was in there for hours. I was in a mess and really thought I was going to lose my thumb, but it was saved. I couldn't go to work for months after and I had to have physio on my thumb. Even today it still isn't right; I have one thumb shorter than the other and can't straighten it.

And, because I was young and growing up, I suppose that's why I still stayed with him. Yet he made me feel an abomination. He used to really put me down and make me feel even more worthless than my dad did.

Yet he didn't want me to be with anyone else, so he would buy me food – and I would just eat. He would buy me fish and chips, then get me some chocolate, then a Chinese – all in one day.

The amount of calories I must have consumed!

I think there is a theory about people who do this – It's called the 'feeder theory'.

A feeder is someone who is a control freak. They are not in control of their own lives so they need to control someone else's, so they find someone vulnerable, perhaps with body dysmorphia or needing to be loved. And they usually control them with food. 95 per cent of feeders are men; in fact I don't know any women who do it. And the woman is so insecure she will do anything to stay with that man.

The only way the man can control that person (but not love them) is to make them so big that they become dependent on the man for food and attention. This happens especially in the USA where people get so big they are bed bound. And it's all a control thing. The feeder doesn't want to lose what they have got, but doesn't know how to keep that person any other way. The only way is to completely overtake their lives. That is what he was doing to me: controlling me by making me bigger and bigger because he knew I had no self confidence – and he didn't want to lose the financial side of what he got from me. There was never any love.

If you feel as if someone is controlling you, just try and step back and take a look at your life and what you are letting someone do to you; someone else ruling your life and taking it away from you. You can't allow that to happen – you only have one life. You can't allow anyone to change you: they accept you as you are or not at all.

You have to find your strength and say: "Actually no. I don't need you making me feel worthless and insecure."

You need to be with someone who wants to be with you because of who you are.

And you might not do this today, or tomorrow. But say to yourself: "I damn well will walk and go. Fuck it. I will stand on my own two feet and I will come out the other side and be happy."

And you will.

You have to find that inner strength from somewhere. And you do find it somehow, but you only seem to find it just when you need it. You can be pushed and pushed and pushed and keep going back until you are pushed so far and can't take any more.

And that is the day you move on and live for yourself – not for anyone else.

Mr Green took all my wages off me every week. I was like a bank to him.

I used to stay at his house. We would fall out then there would be a bit of a reprieve.

Meantime my own mum and dad were falling out and mum was at the end of her tether, on the point of a nervous breakdown. Mum had moved back home by now because she could not live away from her home anymore. After all, it was her house.

I saw what my mum went through and just thought that was how it is. I just saw all men as wankers.

I wondered: 'Are all men like this? Do they all cheat and hurt you? Do they all have lots of girlfriends and want you to be upset?' All I was brought up with was my mum being unhappy. I didn't know what a normal relationship was.

On my brother Darryl's wedding day I was bridesmaid. The bride Dawn was 6ft tall with a supermodel body, tall and thin with beautiful bone structure. She was absolutely stunning: like Claudia Schiffer.

I was this big fat frump and I was so jealous of how beautiful Dawn was. I wanted to be like her because she was so pretty. We went for a dress fitting. She was size eight or ten; her cousin Helen was an eight, really skinny and pretty, looking beautiful in a blue satin dress. I wanted to look like that, but I was fat and ugly with horrible vile hair.

My dress was a size 16 – and it was still too small, so they put me in an 18. Helen laughed at that, but not to be nasty. She just thought it was funny.

But that gutted me to the core.

I didn't want to be a bridesmaid because I was so embarrassed. I thought I would ruin their day and spoil their photographs – and that was the last thing I wanted. At the time I didn't know why I hated myself so much because dysmorphia was not known. I could not bear this vile monster, this gorgon that was me. I reminded myself of Grotbags the big, green, fat, ugly witch in the '80s children's programme Emu's World. But I used to eat all the time. I would tell myself to stop doing something, but still do it. I still do that now. I knew I shouldn't be eating chocolate and bags of chips from the chip shop, but I just could not stop eating. I hated myself that much.

At this stage in my life I didn't even want anyone to like me; it was just a part of my life when the depression of dysmorphia got me down so much I didn't want any attention of any sort from anyone. I just wanted to lie in bed and watch the telly and eat, and hide myself away from the world.

So there was this beautiful bride and stunning bridesmaid – and me – this vile prat with a great big nose and bushy hair. I couldn't wait for the wedding to be over so I could go and get changed into something I could feel more comfortable in. So on my way home to get changed I just cried, and certainly did not want to go back to the reception, but I had to.

I remember going to Skegness with Mr Green. By this time I weighed about 15–16 stones. He was eight stones – and he told me to wear shorts because it was hot. But I think the real reason was he wanted people to ridicule me and laugh at me because of my size.

So I walked along holding his hand: a big fat elephant with a twig. He was so lucky to be thin.

He was very white with black hair and you could see his blue veins. He was wearing shorts, socks and trainers. He did look a twat – but I looked a bigger twat.

We stayed at Richmond Park where my brother had bought my Mammar and Grandad's old caravan. One day we had a terrible row in the caravan. I can't remember whether it was over money or sex (I was never a sexual person because I hated my body). He pushed me on the bed and punched me in the face. Immediately the pain was horrific. He had punched me so hard my nose broken and was just pouring with blood. My eyes came up like balloons in seconds. Then he just drove off – left me – locking me in the caravan and taking the keys.

I couldn't get out of the caravan because the windows were so little. I had no pain killers, no cold compress and the pain was unreal. I just spent my time crying and wiping my nose on a wet towel. I just had to sit and wait for this wanker to come back – not knowing if he even would.

It was dark when he did return hours later (drunk). I tried to get out of the caravan but he wouldn't let me. I tried to get the keys out of his coat pocket but he just grabbed me, so I had to stay the night. He slept in front of the caravan door until the morning.

He never said he was sorry. In fact I think he took great pleasure in seeing me like that.

The reason I carried on with him at all was because I never thought I was worthy to be with a normal person, someone who wouldn't hit me.

As we drove back home I just cried and cried. Even as we were driving along he kept punching me, lashing out to stop me from crying. He dropped me off at the bottom of my road where he chucked my stuff out of the car.

That was the end of that relationship.

My nose did heal, but it was crooked. And it was already crooked from when the girl head butted me at school.

Mum saw the mess I was in. My parents always knew when I was in violent relationships, but they never did anything about it. They thought if I didn't want to be in these situations I would get out. And they were preoccupied with their own marriage breakdown.

Mr Green had been so abusive he had completely stripped every ounce of confidence I had. I knew I just could not carry on with him anymore. When we split up he wasn't bothered anyway because he was already seeing someone else. He was bothered because of the money though.

# Hating Myself

With Body Dysmorphia there is a part of your brain that loves you. There are different parts of the brain, but with dysmorphia the part of the brain that hates you outweighs the part of your brain that loves you 100–1. (It's a part of your make up like with gay men having more hormones than testosterone.)

And it doesn't matter what other people tell you; you feel like a leper and you don't want to inflict your ugliness on other people, which makes you a recluse a lot of the time. It's like being back in the dark ages and you don't feel like part of normality. And you don't want to inflict your ugliness on people, not wanting to offend them. I would not wish dysmorphia on anyone. I did try counselling, but unfortunately it did not work for me. I think it could help others, but I just deal with my dysmorphia my way. I might have a good day, a good week. I can even have a pretty day – no, actually, I don't.

But throughout all my early years I was bullied for the way I looked.

I was bullied because I was skinny so I put weight on – then I was bullied because I was fat. If it wasn't because of that it was because of my nose or because I was poor. When I look back I believe I was ugly – but I was dysmorphic as well.

Dysmorphia is not just wanting people to tell you that you are beautiful. It is a crippling mental ailment. You can look alright on the outside to people, but hate everything about yourself, even your skin and everything that runs through the system.

Some people hate their skin so much they cover themselves with tattoos or piercings – or they scar themselves on purpose just so their skin is not naked. There are so many different strains of dysmorphia.

"How is anyone ever going to want to talk to me, spend their life with me?" I wondered. Nobody knows what goes on in somebody else's head. Nobody can know, because they are not that person.

I was still allowing myself to be controlled as a result of the lack of love and cuddles from my dad. I now had Mr Green controlling my future. And he was also controlling in a different way – controlling what I ate.

I was trying to take control, but even when I was thin I still saw myself as fat, and still do today. Even now I think I am the same size I was when I was 20 stones. I see what I see and can't stop what is going on in my head. I don't care what you tell me; it's what I see. I know that I am not AS big, but I know I am STILL big. People still make comments about me being big, in the papers for example. They might think it's funny, but they don't understand how mentally crippling it is. For a non sufferer it is difficult to explain. You can't just 'pull yourself together'. For me it's not manageable. To a certain degree I can control it a little, but then I'll have an eruption which brings it all back. I do try, but people just think I'm mental.

I am so bad some days I don't actually want to be alive any more.

And without my son H, my mum, Rich, and my best friends, Jade and Janey (more about them later) I would have killed myself. H is really understanding. He tells me I am beautiful all the time and if I want surgery he says 'whatever you want done'.

I'm happier now, the most content in my life, not physically, but with material things. I have three of the best friends in the world, my son, my mum and my dogs – but physically and emotionally I am a wreck.

A lot of dysmorphia sufferers find it hard to be in a relationship because to keep that feeling inside yourself is disabling. Sometimes you don't even want to get out of bed – because you're going to see a reflection of yourself.

If I brush my teeth in front of the large mirror in the bathroom I just sit on the bath and cry, ashamed of myself.

But I know I have got to pull myself together for H.

Years ago I used to be a complete and utter wreck because I could not control my dysmorphia; nothing could make it alright. When I have a good day I am still ugly, but not that bad. But if I catch sight of my reflection it completely throws me: the cellulite in my arms or my stretch marks. I hate my blue eyes, so I wear brown contact lenses a lot. Years ago my next door neighbour told me I have the eyes of a devil.

"Only devil's children have blue eyes," he said – and I've hated them since. That's still with me 30 years later.

# Mr Blue

After splitting up with Mr Green I met someone else – who I'll call Mr Blue.

This was the first person I ever actually lived with. This was about 1988/89 and we bought a house in Bullwell, still in Nottinghamshire.

I was 18, still working at Speedo.

There was a girl I worked with whose fella's best friend was Mr Blue. She set us up on a blind date. Even though I was really fat Mr Blue didn't see it as an issue because he had a sister who was big. He was a virgin, only ever had one girlfriend before.

He was 6ft 2in, ever so gorgeous, really cute with jet black spiky hair – and really muscular.

I never thought in a billion years anyone like that would be interested in me. I thought all my Christmases had come at once.

Because he was a virgin and I was giving him lots of attention I think he liked it. And we did get on really well. But because I didn't like me, I couldn't see how he could.

At the time I was still physically addicted to food, unable to stop eating even though I wasn't hungry. I wouldn't stop eating until my stomach felt really hard.

I'm not sure whether Mr Blue started seeing me only because I was someone he could take the piss out of. But he said he liked me anyway.

I remember feeling really self-conscious because my legs were so big. This was one of the first times I actually began hurting myself. I used to punch myself or hit myself with objects because I was so ugly. I'd try to exercise but couldn't because I never had the willpower then, but couldn't. Even though I hated the way I looked I still couldn't motivate myself. I am only 5ft 'n' a fart, so to be 16 stones, in a size 16–18 in the 1980s, was big.

I never had the confidence to be naked with him, so it was about a month or two before we did anything.

I met him in June 1988 and by November '88 we bought the house having only known each other for five months.

During the first few months he didn't want me to be thin. But gradually he started making comments like 'if you lose a few pounds you would look a lot nicer' or 'I think you should change'. He would suggest I do my hair or make-up differently.

I hated everything about myself – from my hair, my nose, my face (the bane of my life). But there was nothing I could do. My nose had already been broken once by Mr Green; and fractured when I was at school.

We had a great big mirror in the house, but I hated to look at myself in it. There was nothing I could find nice about me. My feet were too small and too fat. I had fat fingers, a fat arse, huge chunky thighs, man's hands – and no tits.

I knew he was embarrassed to be seen with me so I used to try and squeeze myself into clothes which were too small so he didn't know how big I really was.

As he was a body builder he wanted to get bigger so he started injecting steroids. Perhaps he was also suffering from BDD, but he never knew either.

I loved the way he looked, but I was petrified of him when he was on steroids because of the monster they turned him into. Before going on steroids he was really placid and easy going but when he started to take them he got really bad spots on his back and his moods were unbelievable.

Jesus Christ, the mood rages were absolutely unreal. He was like the Tasmanian devil.

He would go into a rage and push me on the floor if his food wasn't cooked right, if he had had a bad day, or if I hadn't got the right food from shopping. At first he would smash the house up in one of his rages then go to bed.

But then he started to grab me and shake me vigorously, and push me into walls and doors. And by this time he was about 20 stone of solid muscle.

He would slam doors on me, slap me on the back of the head, pull my hair, kick me – then go to sleep and wake up fine.

When he was off steroids he wasn't vile, just a miserable human being. But I don't know if the steroids turned him into that. All he wanted to do was sleep and moan – about money, the house, the garden or telling me I'd got to do this or that.

I used to think 'Christ almighty, I'm 20 years old here. Give me a break!'

From the age of about 19–22 I was like a prisoner in my own home. I was young and worked, but he would come home, eat then go to sleep. I couldn't do anything because I hadn't got any friends.

I used to do everything for him apart from wipe his arse – and if I'd said I'd do that he would have let me. I even used to put the toothpaste on his brush. I would get up, do his breakfast (even put sugar on his cereal and butter his toast), do the cleaning after work, cook his tea and run him a hot bath.

He would just come home and sleep, unless he was on the doors. He was a doorman at nightclubs, which made me even more paranoid about being this ugly, fat, vile abomination. Being a bouncer he'd have all these lovely skinny women chatting him up. I know he had at least one of them behind my back because I found out later he was shagging his friend's girlfriend. I don't know how many others there were – but he would come home about 6am.

The type of girls he went for had big boobs and were really skinny.

He was always at the gym seeing these skinny, toned, beautiful girls and sometimes he'd come back and say 'so and so's' bird was there and she was dead fit.

He'd never actually say how ashamed of me he was, but he would say: "Don't you think you should lose some weight? What do you think people think of you when you're walking round in those jeans?"

Obviously I was so hideous and I never actually realised how much hatred he had for me.

We used to go to body building competitions and I was this huge fat blob. I used to hate having sex with him because he had this fantastic body and I was so ashamed, not even wanting to get undressed in front of him. I didn't want him to touch this fat blob of a monster, thinking he could do so much better. So I'd just do it, wanting it to be over so I could get dressed again. Or I'd argue on purpose, make out I was ill, asleep, too tired, having a period – anything so I didn't have to have sex with him.

His mum hated me. She never took to me because he left home to live with me. He was the apple of her eye and I was taking her baby away from her. I was never good enough for her son. She thought I never looked after him properly. His dad didn't like me either – and he knew all about my dad Cliff.

It did used to break my heart, because I saw the real love he got from his parents and I just wanted to be accepted. I hoped I could have had that love from his parents – but I never got it from them either, even though I tried hard with them all the time.

His sister was big as well, about the same size as me. In fact she used to like me when I was big – but not when I started to lose weight.

It was around this time I lost my job. I wasn't turning up because of the bullying at work. On the last day I spent there we were having a stock sale in the upstairs canteen where you could get some cheap seconds. I had bought some stuff and I was on my way out when two machinists and a girl from the office came up behind me and pushed me from the top of the stairs. I fell about half way down the hard metal stairs and they just laughed and laughed. They thought it was really funny. I was in absolute agony, but I never told my boyfriend because I was too embarrassed. I felt as if I had failed again. Everything I wanted to do I failed at and I had failed at my job as well. I was a complete fuckin' failure.

Mr Blue thought I was going to work but I would go to the doctors instead and get signed off sick. Or I would set off, but get the bus back home when I knew he had left for work, then phone in sick. Sometimes I would phone in sick from the payphone near the factory, then go home. But I was worrying myself sick because I knew I would get no money at the end of the week.

I did try to go back, I wanted to go back. I would say to myself 'they are not going to do this to me', but I was too scared.

In the end I got the sack and I was shitting myself worrying he would find out and beat the living crap out of me.

He did find out and he went mad. This was at a time when the mortgage rate was going up and he was going absolutely nuts because we had no money. It took me about a month to get another job.

Some of my past jobs include working in a factory as a packer. I also got a job where I had to use a big steam iron, and at a hosiers putting stockings on a machine. I've also had jobs at a wristband factory – and at an Ann Summers factory which made sexy underwear.

After a month I saw a job advertised as a machinist in a factory where there were older women in their 40s, 50s and 60s. I got the job and was much happier at work. I loved it there.

One day I went home from work and switched on the TV. It was about the early 90s and a chat show was on with Vanessa Feltz, one of the first chat shows to be broadcast on TV I think.

They were showing a woman – how fat she used to be with a cardboard cut-out of her on the stage. And now there was this stick of a woman on stage.

Vanessa said: "This is what she used to look like. And this is what she used to eat."

This woman used to be massive, now she was just a seven to eight stone twig. She looked amazing, fantastic.

Then the programme went on about bulimia, which I had never even heard of. It wasn't something that was ever spoken about then.

That was the very point my life changed.

Vanessa Feltz's show gave me bulimia!

I wonder how many other people the show backfired for. Instead of helping, it assisted instead. It actually guided me through how to be bulimic: eat, drink, then put your fingers down your throat. I never once took the consequences of bulimia on board. I just decided I was going to do it.

I was now only working part time so I would finish about 1pm or 2pm. I would wait until I had finished work, then go to the Co-op and buy a massive family sized cream cake and huge tub of double cream. Then I would walk to Woolworths and get two family sized bars of Dairy Milk. Then I would go to the cob shop and buy cobs, cake and pastries. I would also buy a couple of pints of chocolate milk. Then I'd go home to watch Vanessa Feltz and Take The High Road – while gorging myself. I would eat and eat and eat until I physically could not eat any more – then go to the toilet or the kitchen sink and push my fingers down my throat to make myself throw up.

I spent a fortune on crap just to throw it up down the toilet.

I was weighing myself – and losing weight quickly.

Another subject covered by Vanessa was anorexia and laxative abuse. That was more information for me to take on board so I could lose weight.

I had never been thin since I was little and this was something I desperately needed to be again. I just did not want to look the way I did. I didn't want to be this vile, fat ugly gargoyle. The only way I could make myself feel better was to change me.

I was so unhappy being fat, but I would rather be unhappy and be thin.

Vanessa's show told the story of this woman taking 100 plus laxatives in a day. I thought: 'Hello. I could do that an' all!'

So I would buy packets and packets of laxatives. They were the most vile things, red tablets called Nylax. It was like eating copper. As soon as I took them my mouth filled up with water and I knew I was going to be sick.

And, I have had some horrible things in my mouth, trust me.

But I would eat all my junk – my cakes, cream, cobs and chocolate, then be sick. Then I would drink chocolate milk – and two boxes of laxatives.

I had no energy, but I couldn't care less because I was losing weight.

My mum said I looked really ill – but I took that as a compliment not an insult because I knew I was losing weight. With my bone structure I looked like Skeletor, but I was at the point of my life now when I was actually achieving something for once, even though it was damaging my health.

People say I don't look good thin – but I would sooner look bad and thin than look good and fat.

I was in absolute agony with my teeth. Because I was being sick so many times a day I started to get really bad toothache. I never really thought much about it until one day I could not actually get out of bed because of the pain from abscesses caused by the acid from being sick about 20 times a day.

I couldn't even keep water down. I even got paranoid about how many calories were in the laxatives! If I had had a knife in bed I would have slit my wrists because of the pain.

I knew what pain was like, having suffered a broken nose. But this was unbelievable agony. My mouth was throbbing; so was my nose, my cheek, my eye.

Because I couldn't get up I had to wait for Mr Blue to come home to take me to the emergency dentist. Because of my bulimia the acid had worn the enamel off my teeth.

The gums were so inflamed I could not even put my teeth together because of the abscesses.

The dentist flicked my top tooth and I just screamed in agony.

He had to drain an abscess by putting a hole in the back of my tooth to draw the puss out. He could not numb the pain so I had to have it done without anaesthetic. I have never been in such excruciating agony. The dentist had to remove the nerves; my teeth were completely fucked.

I didn't tell the dentist I was bulimic but he asked me if I was sick a lot. He told me: "If you're making yourself sick, always drink milk before and after."

He explained how the calcium helps rebuild the enamel on your teeth.

Christ! I was even getting advice from the dentist on how to be bulimic! Obviously lots of people were doing it.

He put me on antibiotics – and even all this didn't stop me.

Then my bum collapsed.

It happened one day when I took loads of laxatives. We were supposed to be going on holiday in two weeks and I was so desperate to be thinner. I was in bed in absolute agony. I tried to get to the toilet because I thought I was going to shit myself. I crawled off the bed and managed to get to the landing where I fell doubled up in pain and just lay there crouched in the foetal position.

I had been taking at least 100 laxatives a day for three months. I was a complete twat. I didn't know what effect they would have on me, all I knew was that I needed to be thin.

I must have fainted because the next thing I knew was waking up two hours later covered in blood and shit. I was a complete and utter mess. It was awful, absolutely unbelievable. Mum took me to hospital – but I signed myself out even while I was on the stretcher (before Mr Blue would find out) and went to the doctor instead. I was so frightened of what Mr Blue would say.

I needed to get home so I could get to the doctor's then clean the blood and shit off the carpet because Mr Blue would have gone mad. When he came home I was just trying to clean it up. I blamed the cat, said it had shit all over the carpet. Anyway, we had to have a new carpet – and he never did find out what really happened, well, you do now – sorry luv!

My bowels had ruptured and my colon had deteriorated so much that everything had come out through its wall. Since then I never have been able to shit properly. I can eat and it will take me months before I go to the toilet.

TV's Gillian McKeith says you should go every day. I'm lucky if I go twice in six months despite eating me greens! And it all stems back to that day years ago. Even today I never go to the toilet without laxatives.

Later in life the specialist told me I need surgery. But I never went back because I was too frightened. Even though I love plastic surgery nowadays (you do that for yourself) I hate going to hospitals for 'proper surgery'.

No matter how much you think you are not doing your body any harm, laxatives do deteriorate the bowel and colon.

Anyway, despite what happened, we went on holiday to Tunisia with our best friends at the time. I weighed about seven to seven and a half stones. Our friend was bigger than me – with huge tits, so I was really paranoid about her. I could see Mr Blue looking at her all the time. She was stunning and I was this horrid thing. Even though I was thin I had no boobs, was so ugly and had awful hands and feet. I had stretch marks from when I was fat (which he used to point out) and cellulite. He took great pleasure telling me I had the most horrendous legs he had ever seen in his life.

The holiday was awful. It was baking hot, in the 90s – but I would always cover up, wear cardigans and loads of make-up. It could have been such a lovely holiday, but I didn't want people looking at me in a bikini. If I wore a bikini I would lie down so people wouldn't see me. I would always wear make-up and cover myself up even when sunbathing.

When I heard our friend was going topless I cried all day because I knew my man would see what it would be like to have a real girl (she never did though, thank God).

Back home I got obsessed with exercise and weights and turned the spare room into a gym.

Then came the day I first saw Pamela Anderson on TV's Baywatch which had a huge effect on me. She had the biggest impact on my life as far as body image is concerned.

As soon as I saw her I instantly knew that that was the way I needed to look – and I knew that plastic surgery was now available to make yourself look the way you want. Everything was just perfect: her hair, face, boobs, body, legs and tan.

I had always idolised Samantha Fox, Dolly Parton, glamour girls from the '80s and the comedian Faith Brown who had the biggest boobs I had ever seen in my life. To me, they all looked like dolls – and everybody seemed to love them and make a fuss of them. I thought this was because of the way they looked: blonde with big boobs.

I kept looking at myself in the mirror and did not want to be alive any more. I know some people will think this is really shallow, but when you suffer from BDD it is a form of obsession.

Before I had even seen Pamela Anderson I had this vision in my head of the way I wanted to look. And this image in my head was her to a certain degree.

At the time I did not understand what the hell was wrong with me.

Also, I was only 21 – and I wanted some attention.

But I wasn't always honest with Mr Blue.

My routine with him was to get up in the morning, cry (because

I could see myself), brush my teeth in bed so I did not have to use the mirror, sit in the spare room putting on so much make-up (foundation, concealer, loads of powder, blusher, mascara – then wipe it off and start again).

I could do this three or four times before starting on my hair.

My hair was horrendous because I had started dying it at such an early age, wanting to be blonde. Bleaching it all the time turned it into a wiry frizz and my hair was snapping off. I had been dying my hair since I was about eight or nine.

I would wash it again and would take hours blow drying it, then the hairdryer would make if frizzy, so I would wash it again.

It could take me a day to get ready.

If we went anywhere I would just sit in the car and start arguments or make excuses so I wouldn't have to even get out of the car because I hated the way I looked.

I should have been more honest with him.

When I lost weight I would dress like Pamela Anderson – in a swimsuit and cut-off jeans. Mr Blue's family never liked the way I dressed and his sister started to really despise me because I had lost so much weight – while she had gained a lot. She was a real nasty bitch to me.

Although Mr Blue was a pain in the arse and violent it was only down to the steroids. I think he really was a nice down to earth guy, a lovely guy – one of the best I have ever met.

I was with him for about three or four years.

But because I was always being left on my own day after day I just needed attention. And the attention I got was from his fat sister's husband – who I'll just call Mr Black.

Trust me. This man was angry.

# Mr Black

He was about nine or ten years older than me. At first he just used to be nice to me and say he would look after me and never hurt me. He used to take me out, which was great because much of my life with Mr Blue was spent stuck indoors. Even when we went on holiday he'd just sleep and not do anything.

Mr Black told me his marriage was over and I believed him. He said they didn't have sex. I thought she was quite a nasty person anyway. So to start with I was just enjoying spending time with him. We would spend the day together, but we were not being close.

After a few months of being close friends with Mr Black he said he had had enough of his wife and did not want to be with her anymore. He said he wanted to be with me, so he was going to leave his wife.

I was not in love with Mr Blue anymore; he was just someone I lived with – and I had started to feel differently about him. I didn't like the way he was with me. I already hated myself, but for God's sake, he would pick on things which made me feel even more inferior. He would go on about my front teeth, which had gone black because I was suffering from bulimia. He would say I was flabby with no tits – that was all I used to get from him.

Because Mr Black's wife was heavily overweight he didn't put me down to start with. But then, why would you if wanted to have an affair with someone?

The day came when he said he was going to leave his missus – then he changed his mind. But it was too late anyway. My boyfriend and his wife had already worked out we were seeing each other.

So I moved out of my house at Bullwell and he left his. He moved back in with his parents.

A lot had been going on with my mum and Cliff (my dad) while all this was going on and they too had split up by this time, so I moved back in with my mum.

Our Darryl was married by this time with baby Ashley.

Me and Mr Black had only been together for just two days when he popped out saying he was going to the chip shop – but he was gone for hours.

There was a pay phone at the bottom of the road and my head was telling me he would be there. It was pissing down with rain but I ran from the house to the phone, with nothing on my feet – and I saw his car outside the phone box.

I cried so much I could hardly breathe. I opened the phone box door and he was on the phone to her. He put the phone down and he said to me: "I'm going back to her. I want her back."

He said he had made a mistake and did not want to be with me. I went home and cried and cried and cried. He did not even want a divorce.

I managed to go back to work – and a week later he told me he was sorry, he loved me and wanted me back.

So I always had this feeling that I was second best with Mr Black. After all, he didn't really want me. He had gone back to his wife, who he told me treated him like shit, and she didn't want him. I didn't even like him anymore.

And I had lost everything. I had sacrificed everything for this man who I thought liked me.

I was an independent woman with my own property – and just walked away from it. I had signed everything over to Mr Blue because I felt so guilty. He also kept the savings, the furniture, the lot.

All I had ever done was be nice to Mr Black. What had I done wrong?

It seemed to me that obviously, if he had wanted to go back to someone he used to call Grotbags, then I must be really ugly and vile. He went back to this woman he said he despised and hated. They tried for about a week then she told him she didn't want him back.

So he moved in with me at mum's for a few months and we slept on a single bed. I still didn't love this guy, but I did have feelings for him at the beginning I suppose.

Then I got pregnant, even though we were using a condom – so I know my son H was meant to be, thank God. I just knew I had made my son that night. I knew I was pregnant.

I was 24 and frightened about being pregnant, but never contemplated getting rid of the child. I was with a man I didn't trust because I knew all his ex-wife had to do was click her fingers and he would go back, even though she had divorced him.

Mum said I couldn't have a baby out of wedlock, so we arranged to get married.

But when I was only two or three months pregnant I had a taste of things to come.

Mr Black was a stupid car fanatic. He had this Golf GTi which he had crashed and then the beginning of the year rebuilt, but there was no heater in it.

It was January, freezing cold, sleeting and snowing.

Mr Black said he was going to see a mate who worked in a car stereo shop. He left me outside in the car saying he would be ten minutes, but I was left there for hours, pregnant with no heating.

Eventually, frozen, I went into the shop and asked if he could hurry up.

He came out, got in the car with me and drove off.

Then he stopped the car, punched me in the face and said: "Don't you ever do that to me again. Don't you ever humiliate me."

I got out of the car but he dragged me back in again and drove off. He punched me in the chest and shouted things like: 'Who do you think you are?' and 'You know your place'.

The punch gave me a huge black eye, and because we were still living at mum's he told me to say I had walked into a door. So that's what I told mum and she didn't question it.

I can't hand on heart say I was ever in love with this man; I was just trapped because I was pregnant. And I felt I would rather have committed suicide than have an abortion. I was 24 years old and had lost everything, but I knew I wanted this baby. I thought that if I stayed with this man, at least this baby would have some sort of life. I wanted my child to have a mum and dad who loved him. But I didn't realise just how vile Mr Black could be; he was never right with me and I was always on edge.

He was not a calm person, was quite erratic and obsessed with cars – I mean obsessed to the point of it being abnormal.

But we started looking for a house and eventually bought one. I was still suffering badly from BDD but I stopped taking laxatives because of the baby. I was a tiny size eight at this time and knew I had to eat for the baby's sake, but I also knew I would gain weight.

I stopped working when I was about three or four months pregnant.

I had 'morning' sickness which lasted 24 hours so I would eat, then be sick.

But within the first month of being pregnant I had gained a stone. Then I just got bigger and bigger and bigger.

Remember, he only wanted to be with me because his ex-wife was so large, so even though I was only getting bigger because I was carrying his child he resented it.

And as I got bigger he got more aggressive.

He was mentally abusive while I was pregnant, saying really nasty things.

"Look at you," he'd say. "If you get any bigger..."

I went from eight to 15 stones. I was gigantic – with the baby and fat. (Mum says she went up to 19 stones carrying me!).

So at some point I stopped eating again, thinking there was at least fat to keep the baby going. Mum knew I had stopped eating and she went crazy.

The problem is, if you stop eating, when you start eating again you gain weight three times as fast as a healthy person's body. The weight goes on immediately because your body is so starved.

Mr Black was a complete control freak. I always knew that when he was with his ex-wife their house was always immaculate and I thought that was down to her – but it was him. He was fanatical about things being straight, tidy and clean, even in cupboards and under the sink.

Although I was heavily pregnant I would clean the house from top to bottom, cook his tea, do the garden. (I was interested in starting a business in landscape gardening so I wanted my garden to look perfect so I could take photos of it to show people.)

In our house everything had to be in order in the cupboards and Mr Black would know if there was a fingerprint on the TV. He even used to brush the fringes on the rugs so they would be straight.

I watched a film once called Sleeping with the Enemy and thought 'Oh my God, that's him. They have made a film of him, a complete and utter control freak'.

He wouldn't even let me drive. All he cared about was his mates, his TV and his car. He never came with me to see the midwife or anything.

When I was about six months pregnant, just two days before we got married, I hadn't left the towels straight or something, so he kicked me and hit me on the back of the head. The blow just came out of the blue so I had no time to cradle myself as I fell.

I fell forward onto my stomach and I was petrified the baby was damaged because of how hard I fell.

But he showed no remorse – just fucked off with his mates.

I was about 20–22 stones and had a 62 inch waist. The stretch marks were so bad they used to bleed because my skin could just not stretch any more. People were convinced I was having quads.

It was a really hot summer in 1995, one of the hottest I could remember. I would sweat so much under my arms and my boobs – and I ended up with open sores at the top of my legs where they had rubbed together.

I was a size 24 so could not find pants to fit me as they wouldn't stay up on my lump, so I walked around with no knickers on. I was so paranoid about my weight that I would walk around in huge cardigans and massive coats, passing out all the time with the heat.

On the morning of the wedding I didn't want to marry him. I sat there on my own while he was pissing about with his car on our wedding day. While I was doing my hair and actually asked myself 'What am I doing?'

We had a row that morning and he said he was not going to marry me. I said: "Whatever."

I spent the morning crying because I did not want to marry him.

My outfit was horrendous, like a tent. I was 22 stones and looked awful. We got married at Nottingham Register Office at the beginning of August – not the beautiful fairytale wedding I had dreamed of in a church.

I later found out he shagged my best mate on my wedding night. He gave her a lift home with the wedding gifts still in the boot of the car. It seems she was only my best friend because she was shagging my husband.

My wedding day, from start to finish, was the worst day of my life when it should have been the happiest.

I will never know the feeling of dad walking me down the aisle, for dad to say 'you are my princess'; and to have your husband at the end of the aisle wanting you because of who you are and wanting to marry you, giving his life to spend with you and no other woman.

All that has been taken away from me. Even if I was to marry again it would be my second marriage. So my dream was destroyed. This is not what every little girl, even in her teens, dreams of. It was not what I wanted.

Throughout my pregnancy the midwife had reassured me, because I was so petrified, saying: "You never have to worry about having a baby unless your waters are brown."

I should have had my baby on 11th September, on my birthday, but he was late, so I was due to go to hospital to be induced on 29th September. But on 28th September I had awful pains and was being so sick, even though I had not eaten from Monday to Thursday that week. (Mr Black was watching Top Gear as usual, then he was going to go out and get a Chinese.)

I told him: "I think I am having the baby."

"Don't be so stupid," came the reply.

Then I had the worst pain and I jumped off the sofa. The water just gushed out of me onto the carpet and he went absolutely nuts.

The water was brown…

"You selfish fuckin' cow!" he yelled (because he wanted to watch TV).

I was screaming because I had been told if the water was brown the baby would be in distress.

He went to fetch tea towels and gave them to me so I could sit on them in his car. Although it was only September it was really cold and foggy. He ushered me into the car and took me to hospital.

I was in labour from 8.30pm that Thursday night until 12.30pm Friday. Mum was with me but he went home 'to go to sleep' – but he was shagging that girl again while I was giving birth to his child.

He was there when I actually gave birth – but only in body, not mind, as he didn't want to be there.

During the birth I was screaming at the nurse telling her I knew I was ripping, and my mum told her. But the midwife said I had to push as H had got stuck. I was already weak and tired because

I hadn't eaten all week. And because H was lodged they could not get forceps on him to get him out. The midwife said if I did not push I would suffocate my child, so even though I knew I was tearing I had to push.

When H was born he had the cord wrapped round his neck twice, he was not breathing and he was blue. They put a tube down his throat, but he still didn't cry so he was rushed to intensive care.

For ten hours no one told me whether my baby was alive or dead. I didn't even know if the baby was a boy or girl.

I had to have stitches because of the tear – but instead of doing the inside stitches first they did the outside first. I felt every stitch of the inside ones. So every time I had an inside stitch the outside stitch would tear. I lost so much blood I had to have a transfusion.

Ten hours after the birth Mr Black came back with a Polaroid picture of the baby and chucked it at me.

"Is it dead?" I asked.

"No, he's alive."

"Oh, is it a boy?"

He then told me H was really ill and his lungs had flooded with meconium.

Never in my life had I been so frightened, because I really thought I was going to lose him.

The nurse wouldn't let me see him, but Mr Black actually cried when he saw H because he was so tiny – 10lbs – but so tiny.

His lungs had badly flooded and his ears were defective. Even today H has problems with his inner ear. Sometimes he's OK, but other times he has problems with noises.

The insensitive bastards at the hospital put me in a postnatal ward. It was horrible to see all those mums with their babies, nursing them and cuddling them while H was in intensive care for five days where I couldn't cuddle him.

I found it difficult to bond with H because I suffered from postnatal depression, maybe because I didn't have those first few seconds with him. At first I didn't realise I had postnatal depression. I tried to breastfeed H but couldn't because my milk had dried up so I had to bottle feed. I wanted to breastfeed so my baby would be a part of me, as if I was keeping him alive by giving him part of me.

As well as postnatal depression, my BDD was very bad at this point.

I used to pick up H, but never felt close to him which made me feel frustrated with myself and I became really depressed. I would listen to him crying and I would get out of bed, but I would have to make myself.

And Mr Black was not the best dad in the world. He would change a nappy sometimes, but mostly I was on my own with the baby.

H was a crying baby. This wasn't his fault as he was very poorly. But he would cry and cry and cry. When it got to the point when I could not stand it anymore I would just scream and scream so loud in the conservatory.

But when he was asleep I could see this defenceless baby and I wanted to hug him.

The doctor put me on anti-depressants, on Prozac, which made me worse, made me suicidal.

Coping with a baby, a man I did not want to be with and dysmorphia all really got on top of me and I really don't know how I pulled myself out of it.

When H was about five or six months Mr Black would come and go, here and there. When he was about a year old my ex would mostly say: "Oh for God's sake will you shut that kid up. How many times have I told you?"

He'd say he was trying to watch TV.

So I used to sit upstairs in the bedroom with H. I loved him so much and we spent so most of our time together there, but it took me about six months to feel that way.

By the time H was around a year old Mr Black's temper was flaring up all the time. He would grab me and punch my arm, or when we were sitting on the sofa he would thump me in the leg. He would say he was messing about but he wasn't because he would do it so that it would hurt.

Nothing I did pleased him. No matter what I tried to do he was not happy with me. I hadn't cooked this right or the house wasn't tidy or the garden looked a mess. I did have some good times with him, but these were counteracted 1,000 times over by the bad times. If I had a good hour, we would have ten bad days.

I was just a stepping stone for him to get out of a miserable marriage. But in the marriage he was in before he could not do what he wanted to do. With me he did. He would go out with his mates or with women. In fact he had more respect for his ex-wife, who he was with for about two years, than he did for me.

He was so ashamed of me being fat, so he kept going on all the time: "You're disgusting, you're fat, you're fat, you're fat, lose weight, you are ugly," day after day.

"Every time you put something in your mouth you make me feel physically sick," he'd say.

I would cook dinner and he would say: "You shouldn't eat that. You are so fucking fat."

So, I stopped eating. I developed a really bad food phobia because he had drilled it into me that I would make people feel physically ill if they saw me eating. I would drink water and have about a quarter of an apple each day, or sometimes just one glass of water a day.

While I was with Mr Black there were other family problems to deal with.

One day me and Mr Black had a huge argument so he wouldn't let me use the car to take mum shopping. It was pouring down with rain but mum told me on the phone she would go to the Post Office to get her pension. I told her not to and said I would get a taxi because I had a really bad feeling something was going to happen but she said she would go anyway.

I pleaded with Mr Black: "Please let me take her. Mum is going to get wet through."

So when the phone rang a bit later I instantly knew something had happened. People can say 'what a load of bollocks' but my heart just sank. I knew it was bad news.

It was my Mammar. She told me mum had been mugged.

I was so angry I punched my ex, grabbed H and the car keys and drove straight to see mum.

She was in such a mess.

Mum had walked to the Post Office in the rain. When she came out she was struggling to put her umbrella up; she was in her late 60s/early 70s at the time and really skinny. A black guy tried to cut her bag off her shoulder, but stabbed her in her side.

She got up and chased after him!

There was a car waiting for him with another guy in. It seems they had been targeting pensioners in the area. They had already mugged two OAPs and a blind man. But mum has such a temper; she didn't think about the pain she was in. She ran after this guy, who was between 20–30, to get her handbag back – because it had a Polaroid picture of H in from when he was in the incubator.

The window was down on the guy's car, so she put her hand in to try and get her bag. But they wound the window up and drove off, dragging mum along the road. Eventually she fell on to the road when they released her arm, but they had dragged mum right down the road. There was a car coming the other way, but by sheer luck it stopped. Mum managed to get up and get help. Then she carried on walking – with a broken ankle. She had no skin on her leg, elbows or forearm; her face was grazed and her nose was broken. When I saw her I have never ever cried as much. I was just so hurt to see my mum like that. I phoned the police and took her to hospital.

Unfortunately this led to a huge row between me and my brother Robert.

My brother and his family had issues with mum because they wanted her to leave my dad. He knew Cliff was having affairs when my brothers were little. Mum kept saying she would leave him, but would end up back with him and Robert could not cope with it.

But when mum was mugged Robert didn't get in touch with her at all. I saw Robert with his wife and daughter when I went shopping at Tesco, so I stopped my car and ran up to him.

"Why haven't you phoned your mum?" I asked. "It's our mum. Don't you care?"

To which his daughter replied: "She deserves it."

She was a teenager with the 'so what, we don't care' attitude.

So I punched her and knocked her out.

My brother, who used to be a boxer, then punched me – breaking my nose and blacking my eye. I suppose he was defending his daughter.

To this day we don't speak. I see him when I am shopping and want to speak to him but am scared he is going to dismiss me. I do love him and miss him. I used to love going to his big house in the countryside where he had a big slobbery dog called Blue Boy. I used to love playing with their daughter Hayley's dolls.

I really love my brothers – and would do anything to have a cuddle from them, just once, before it is too late.

Poor mum also had other problems during this time.

Since Gang Gang died me and mum went round to Mammar's often. Over about ten years we would take her out all the time shopping, to lunch or on day trips, do her cleaning and I would do her garden. I would take Mammar's to mum's house for Sunday dinner and pick her up in the week. Mum would take her on holiday. We were all very close and me and mum were always there for Mammar – because we loved her so much. Mammar was always dressed nice, always with her hair done and make-up on.

Mammar was like the Queen. We would go on a picnic and she would sit on her rug and insist on having her china cup; she wouldn't drink out of anyone else's.

Even when Mammar was well into her 80s she would always be made up. She had fiery red hair and wore bright red lipstick, bright red nail varnish and loads of make-up.

And she would still wear high heels.

Her dread was dying on her own without looking her best.

She dreaded it so much she would say on a weekly basis: "Don't let me die on my own without my hair and face done."

She would sit on the sofa watching TV at mum's house with her legs crossed.

"Uncross your bloody legs!" mum would shout because Mammar would always moan about her hips and knees. She was lovely.

Me and mum were round her house one day and Mammar accused me of nicking her watch because she couldn't find it. We just couldn't believe it. Mum went mad and said I would never do anything like that.

I said to Mammar: "After everything I have done for you how can you accuse me of stealing from you?"

Then Mammar said the most awful things to mum.

Mum went into Mammar's drawer to look for the watch and found it – but the damage was done.

We felt completely and utterly betrayed. All we had ever done was spoil her.

I was 27 at the time when this was going on.

Mammar could be a cantankerous old bugger at times and would often be moody and shout, but she turned from being a lovely lady to a nasty, hateful person.

There was about 15 years between mum and Lynn her sister and they never got on well. Lynn was treated like the golden child. Although it was mum who looked after Mammar if Lynn called round Mammar would get dead excited. Mammar would make a real effort and spend money on flowers and chocolates for her. She would save her money so she could spend it on Lynn when she called.

Lynn wasn't the only one who took from Mammar. My brother Robert, who was into antiques dealing, would call round and say things like 'this is nice' or 'can I have this' and Mammar would give it to him – whether it was a piece of furniture or a plate and he would give her a fiver.

Sadly Mammar left shortly afterwards to go and live miles away in Leicestershire with Aunty Lynn. That day was the last time we saw her. We had no Christmas cards, no letters, no phone calls, nothing.

I rang Lynn's and asked to speak to Mammar. Lynn's bloke Norman answered the phone and wouldn't let me talk to her. I think Lynn and Robert poisoned Mammar's mind against us. We never saw Mammar again.

I had at least something to cling to while I was with Mr Black. I started a gardening business.

I had always loved gardening, which probably stems back to when I was little. Cliff, loved his gardening too and it was precious time that I could spend with him.

But the business was something I could do for me – and something which Mr Black would have no control over. I used to watch Gardeners' World on TV and read gardening magazines. I designed our own garden and took photos of it which I showed to people. I know everything about gardening and this is something that interests me. We had a friend who wanted his garden done because he saw what I had achieved with ours. And from there the business just snowballed. I was self-taught. I learned everything from books myself.

I did one guy's garden – at a really posh house with a swimming pool. I spent a fortune on plants for the garden and while I was there he used to make advances towards me. I used to take H with me and the guy would play with him in the pool. He would pick him up, chuck him in the pool and spin him round. I would sit and watch thinking 'why are you doing this with my son? His own dad won't do it'. But it was nice to see it enjoying himself.

This guy fell for me hook, line and sinker but he was married – so I left his garden half done and didn't go back.

I used to work about four or five hours a day – plus do everything at home. I would transform a complete and utter jungle into a beautiful garden, then give the client a little book of before and after photos. Apart from giving birth to H that was the only time I felt proud of myself. I used to think 'I've done all that on my own'. Mr Black used to take some of the money I earned from my business, but I kept some back for savings. I have never asked for anything from anyone. I never ask for anything financially – it is always the other way round – me spoiling the man. I have always treated them, whatever they have wanted, from cars to holidays – just wanting to make them happy. Even now I can't take gifts off people; I get more enjoyment buying things for others with my own money. I still enjoy gardening when I get time.

But while I was working on my business I was lifting some really heavy rockery stones and putting them into a sack. I stood up and my back cracked. I had to see a chiropractor who cracked it back into place – which was awful. The pain was unreal.

So about four or five weeks later we went on a family holiday to Majorca to help me recover and we took my mum.

Me and mum have been inseparable in adult life. I love her more than life itself.

We were on holiday sitting at the side of the swimming pool, Mr Black covered in suntan oil while I sat really self conscious. There was a beautiful woman there (I was still about a size 16) and I caught him looking at her all the time which made me feel so insecure and worthless. He would always turn and look at other women and make comments. There were topless girls there – and I could see he was getting movement in his trunks. That just freaked me out completely, but I still didn't say anything to him. I couldn't swim at the time (I used to be a brilliant swimmer until some kids held me under water) so mum took H in the pool. But mum wasn't very well and H didn't want to come out so I asked Mr Black to go in the water with him. But he would never play with H or give him piggy backs or anything like that.

Anyway he seemed to have a real major strop on with me and I must have told him to fuck off or something before I went to get H out of the pool. Me, mum and H went back up to our room and Mr Black followed us up about an hour later.

"Don't you EVER fuckin disrespect me again," was the first thing he said when he came into the room. "Who do you think you are?"

Then he started calling me a psycho bitch. All this because I had asked him to spend time with his child.

Then he punched me in the face in front of mum and H. It all happened so quickly.

We had a studio type apartment with two sofas, a table and four chairs. There was a massive marble and wood coffee table.

And as I fell back I hit the corner of the coffee table with my back. I was in absolute agony and could not even move. Then he kicked me in the back. Mum, who was about 70 years old at the time, tried to stop him so he punched her.

She went to the kitchen and fetched a carving knife – and I think she was going to stab him. She was so angry.

But he fled and we didn't see him all that day and night. Mum never liked him. She always said he had evil eyes – so blue.

I have since asked her why she told me to marry him then and she says she feels guilty about that to this day.

After that attack I couldn't walk for a week. Mum was so upset she cried and eventually I had to have the doctor round.

By June 1999 I was just skin and bone. I had not eaten for three months apart from tiny snippets, then be sick.

I really would have starved myself to death, but a friend would sit with me and make me eat. My bones were sticking out of my arse when I sat in the bath. Mr Black would barge into the bathroom and say: "That's still not enough. I still can't see your bones enough. Look at your tits. You're vile."

He was starving me. He wanted me dead. But so did I. My BDD was at an all-time high. And he knew what buttons to press and how to make me deteriorate mentally and physically.

Mr Black left us for the first time when H was about 18 months old – but he would go, then I would keep having him back.

H was fanatical about Thomas the Tank Engine but Mr Black only allowed him to have his toys in the conservatory, his playroom. The toys were definitely not allowed in the lounge – that was where Mr Black's speakers and telly were, so nothing was allowed in there. That was his room.

One day Mr Black had gone to work and I had taken H on his first trip to McDonald's where they were giving away something to do with trains with the kids' 'happy meal'.

We were having a lovely day. We got home with the meal and H sat on my knee in the lounge with his McDonald's on a red tray with his chicken nuggets, fries and a little pot of tomato ketchup. Thomas the Tank Engine was on TV and we had brought his train track into the lounge.

Then I heard the front door go – and my heart stopped. I thought 'My life is over'.

"Dear God, don't let this be him," I said.

The door opened – and that was it.

I thought 'Oh my God, what the fuck can I do?'

Mr Black went fuckin' mad.

"What the fuck have I told you?" (In front of the baby). Poor H was screaming.

"Don't you ever have that shit in here again."

He kicked the train set and broke it then knocked the food out of our hands up the wall.

While I was cradling H he punched me in the face and I fell on the sofa. He tried to punch me again so I ran upstairs to the bedroom and closed the door. H was sitting on me knee screaming – both of us covered in ketchup and my lip pouring with blood.

I put a chest of drawers up against the door and put my feet against it.

So Mr Black slammed the front door and left.

I phoned his mum and his parents came round. They did not like me at all as they saw me as the reason for the breakup of his marriage. But his dad rang Mr Black's phone and told him to come back now and sort it out.

He did come home and his mum actually slapped him across his face. He was saying he would never do anything like that again and did not know why he had done it.

I really thought he would change. And financially and emotionally I was frightened to leave. I didn't think I deserved anyone else. And at the time the hatred that he had for me was not half as much as I had for myself.

Now, when I look back, I can't believe I am the same person. I can't believe I would allow a man to do that to me: to mentally, physically and emotionally control me. I would put up with it because I hoped it would turn into love – but it never does. Once somebody like that has you and they hate you they will do nothing to stop at destroying you. They need to take their shit out on you. The hatred I felt from him was the worse feeling – to know that somebody you think you love hates you that much. But looking back I did not love my ex-husband.

Cliff found out my ex was hitting me – but did nothing.

The Christmas before Mr Black finally left I had flu and a tummy bug both at the same time. I couldn't eat and lost a stone in that week alone. Still all he would say was: "Every time you try to eat I feel sick."

Despite all this Mr Black was a good dad sometimes I think, but then again what is a good dad? But he left us for good when H was four, then I had to look at how to pay the bills. (After he left he got someone else pregnant.)

The day he left he kicked the shit out of me in front of H. As he was leaving he said: "I'll see you and that bastard child of mine in the gutter."

We were divorced when H was five. Mr Black just walked out of H's life, never paying anything for him. H was at nursery when his dad left so I set up a gardening business.

When H was little his dad would phone and say he wanted to see him at the weekend. H would get so excited and would sit there with his sandwiches and Thomas the Tank engine packed up – then his dad would ring and cancel; or he just wouldn't turn up and I was left to pick up the pieces.

His dad would promise to buy him things then let him down. And when he had another woman with kids he would spoil her children and give H nothing. When he picked H up in the car he would make him sit on the floor while the other kids sat on the seats. H would have to sleep on a lilo at their house.

After seeing what his dad did to me H became very withdrawn and would not speak at all. He started to chew his lips, sometimes that bad they used to bleed and wet the bed. When Mr Black was home if H tried to speak all he heard was: "Fuckin' shut up. I'm trying to watch TV." Poor H was a nervous wreck. If I had been strong enough to have walked away and stick up for us both he would not have gone through that. But I just wasn't and it will haunt me forever what I put my boy through.

Then a male friend said to me: "Why don't you get him a dog? Get him a pup."

I told him I had always loved Staffies and had always wanted a white one. So he found one and bought him for us for Christmas. We called him Reggie – and H seemed to change overnight.

H and Reggie were inseparable. Reggie even slept in H's bed with his head on the same pillow. Reggie would sit there while H had his breakfast or if he was in the bath. It felt as if there was me and my son – and my little furry son. It was all down to Reggie that H started talking, laughing and being a normal little kid again.

But there were other problems. Mr Black had left me in so much debt. Our mortgage was in joint names and he had not paid any bills. He had loans secured on the house – but he had made no payments so it was in default.

I had started to get all these letters with his name on but I just threw them away because at the time I had no idea about the secured loans. But one day a letter came and it said the word 'court' on the envelope so I opened it.

I did not understand the letter so I phoned a friend who told me I needed to see a solicitor. I took the letters to the solicitor and he said: "You are in a mess" or words to that effect.

I had to go to court and the bailiffs started coming day after day trying to get money and take stuff. Every time there was a knock on the door I would sweat and my heart would stop. Me and H would hide.

One day, completely out of the blue, H's dad came banging on the door. He hadn't seen his son for about two years.

H knew the drill when he heard a knock on the door.

"Mum it's the bad men."

"Don't answer the door," I'd say.

"I know…"

I was in the bath and didn't realise who it was at the door. I looked through the curtains and could see a muscular bloke and just thought it was someone who'd got the wrong address. He started to walk away so I went downstairs intending to go down the path and shout after him.

As I went down the path I saw a BMW with blacked out windows about four or five houses away. I got to the bottom of the path – and my ex-husband came running down towards me before I could get back into the house. He poked H and I kept shouting at him to go in the house. I thought he was going to kill me.

H came out with Reggie to protect me. Even at that age, he was only a baby for God's sake. His dad said: "You fat little bastard. You're no fuckin' son of mine. I'm going to firebomb this house with you and that slag of a mum in it."

I knew he meant it, so I left and went to stay at a friend's for a while, then I went back to mum's while the house was being sold.

He had left me £125,000 in debt.

When H was about ten or 12 Mr Black disappeared out of the country and he has never seen him since.

I could have included a lot more, but for the sake of my boy I am lost. But after that day he changed H, and H never wants to ever have contact with his dad ever again.

# Body Dysmorphic Disorder

Even when I was about six or seven I would punch myself and pull my hair because I didn't like the way I looked.

I knew I was ugly – after all I was bullied because I was ugly. Surely if I didn't have a big nose they wouldn't have called me 'big nose' at school.

Right through infants and juniors I hated my hair.

I also hated my cheeks and would pull at them to try and change their shape and colour.

I used to try and stretch my legs because they are so short. I remember watching a Carry On film where a man was being stretched on a rack. That's where I got the idea from.

I used to make our Darryl pull me to see if my arms or legs would get longer.

I had short, fat size one feet so I would wear me mum's size six shoes with loads of socks. No wonder the kids in the street used to take the piss out of me.

I would punch myself in the face and stomach and hit my head on walls. Mum had a big wooden rolling pin which I would use to hit my hips. I hated them because they stuck out when I was little.

In the 1970s and '80s anorexia was now recognised, but dysmorphia has only been recognised in the last few years in the media. Even now people say 'what is BDD?' But they know what anorexia or bulimia is.

In the '80s binge eating was costing me about £50-£60 a week on junk food.

Perhaps this stems back to when I was little, when food was like love. Because I never got love off my dad food was a comfort – a comfort I could control.

Binge eating was like having control. I wasn't going to eat things I didn't like; I was going to eat things I liked – then be sick.

I really believe if I had not seen that Vanessa Feltz programme that day, if I had not come home early and put that channel on, I would have eventually killed myself.

I was meant to see that programme that day. She gave me the insight without which I would not have coped. Seeing that show was fate. It was meant to happen to me.

People would say to me that I was mental and should just stop eating to lose weight, and I did try to eat healthily but I would stick around 16, 17 or 18 stones. I was big – and miserable. Nowadays it is a little easier because you have different healthy stuff available.

But this person in here does not want to be this person out there.

Some people go to counsellors which I did try, but it made me even worse.

To be me means to be trapped with my thoughts and my brain constantly letting my thoughts and my brain constantly telling me I am ugly. I am odious and I am vile. This hole of despair I'm in is so big and deep there will never be an escape for me. I'd wake up during the night and would be crying. Dreams of not being me always haunted me – and still do today. I'd have panic attacks knowing how I looked and they wouldn't stop. My heart would race so fast and I would shake uncontrollably. And this was worse because I knew I could never be at peace with myself. That's why I had to stop it. And, the only way I saw it go, ever, was to stop breathing. Hour after hour, day after day, I have fights with myself in my head. It was driving me mad and it just couldn't stop!

My relationships were doomed and always will be, because of me. I am me and I can't change that, no matter what. I am so insecure, so demanding, and always want and need attention, needing to be held and cuddled, needing someone to make me feel like me. But I ruin everything. I wish I could just pull my stupid brain out and throw it away.

# Mr Blond

From the beginning to the end of our relationship it was all a lie. Looking back on it, none of it was ever true.

I first met him in 1981 when I was only 11 or 12. I was out with friends at a pub in Nottingham (I always looked older than I was and liked to go out and get drunk). The friend I was with was older than me so he got off with her while I kissed his friend.

Mr Blond was ten years older than me and in a band.

That was the first time we met, but I didn't see him again until 1997 when H was a baby. Me and Mr Black were going through hell and our marriage was just about over. We were still together but he was going off with other women. There was nothing left between us and I weighed about five stones by this time; I was so thin.

It was around this time that I decided I wanted a tattoo. I had seen something on TV about henna tattoos. I had a friend who worked in a shop and I asked her if she sold henna. She didn't – but she told me there was a guy across the road from her shop who did henna tattoos.

I remember it was a red hot Saturday afternoon. H was with my mum as she always had him on Saturday afternoons.

The woman who owned the tattoo place told me the tattooist was at the gym, so she rang him and said: "You have a client in."

I sat down in front of this mirror – and I could see down the road in the reflection. There was a guy walking up the road: bleached blond hair, massive, muscular, with a dark tan. He was wearing shorts and a vest. As I watched in the mirror he got closer and closer and my heart started to feel funny. It was really weird watching this man. He came into the shop, looked at me – and that was it. And he always told me he felt the same. I was really nervous at the prospect of him even touching my arm to do the tattoo. He did a henna dragon tattoo on my arm and told me it should last about two weeks – if not I should come back again. He later told me he deliberately watered down the henna so it wouldn't last. So after a few days I had to go back when it came off. He did the tattoo again and this time we got on like a house on fire.

By this time Mr Black had got someone else, which I was grateful for, because it meant he was not spending any time with me. Although I was lonely at least I did not have someone shouting at me.

Mr Blond wanted to meet me for a drink. He told me he was with a girl but there was nothing between them and that he was trying to end it because the relationship was dead, but didn't know how to do it.

At the time I didn't want a relationship; I just wanted someone to talk to so was happy with a platonic friendship.

Anyway, I met him for a drink. I remember I was wearing a short pink cardie and grey trousers. I was leaning forward with my back to the door as he walked in.

"You have got to eat or you are going to die," was the first thing he said.

By this time I was food phobic; I could not even put food into my mouth. I was so frightened of food it gave me panic attacks. My husband had told me often enough about putting food into my mouth – and I didn't want to hear any more nasty things. I knew I was thin; but I didn't know I was ill. I had about a 21–22 inch waist and a size six used to bury me.

Mr Blond bought me a drink and a salad – and he sat there until I ate it.

"I don't care how long it takes you, but you are going to eat," he said.

Each night he would phone me and we would have a real laugh. I knew he was a player because I had friends who told me he used to sleep around. I knew his character, but I just wanted a friend. He was so good looking all he had to do was click his fingers. He was in a band and people thought he was this almighty rock star in Nottingham.

By this time I was still married, but Mr Black had gone.

Then one day it just happened. I saw Mr Blond at a nightclub and went to say hello, but as I leaned up to his ear he turned his head and I felt his breath on my face. Our noses were touching; we were really close, but did not kiss. His mouth was a millimetre away from mine.

The way he looked at me stopped my breath, stopped my heart; my blood was tingling.

I thought at the time I had fallen head over heels in love with him when I first saw him in that reflection; just the image of him walking up the road was enough for my heart to miss a beat. Then to see how he looked at me, I knew I had never, ever felt this before in my life. But looking back now it was not really love. What I have now, to me, is real.

I had still had no self esteem, but at the end of the night I saw him outside the club. We walked down the road together to get a taxi; then he stopped, grabbed my arm, picked me up, plonked me on a wall and kissed me.

After that night I did meet him but we still didn't have sex. He didn't have much money so I would buy him clothes and shoes. Even though he was handsome I wanted him to feel he had self respect with the clothes he wore. I was still doing my gardening business so was OK money wise.

One day he rang me from his flat, still in bed. He told me to come round – and bring him some breakfast in bed.

So off I went, wearing a new dress, with coffee and something for him to eat. When I got there he was still in bed – and that was it.

I held him so tight. I remember him saying: "Well, that's it now isn't it?"

He told me he loved me, as if he really meant it. (I believe at the time he did). But he was in a bad place himself. Even though he is a twat he has no confidence – he gets that from sleeping around.

I was about 26 or 27 at this time. He made me feel nice; he made me feel – fluffy, girlie.

I remember thinking 'this is what it must be like to love someone' and 'this is how I am going to feel for the rest of my life'. I had fallen in love with him and didn't want this feeling to stop.

But he was bullshitting me.

He said there was nothing between him and this girlfriend but there was.

After a few weeks I realised I was pregnant. I was in a mess, a wreck. My ex-husband had gone and I didn't know whether I was going to lose the house – or what my ex was capable of doing. He had already stripped the house of furniture and taken the cars. All I had was dwindling savings.

I'd got H but no stability and I was mentally fucked, an emotional wreck.

People will say 'you should have used protection' etc – but we didn't.

By this time Mr Blond was now telling me he wanted to make it work with his girlfriend and would not leave her, so I didn't tell him I was pregnant. But I was starting to get bigger and bigger and bigger. One day I went to his place and he said: "You are getting really big; you are putting a lot of weight on." It was then I told him I had been for tests and I was pregnant.

"Well it ain't mine," was his reply.

He thought I was trying to trap him and the relationship was ruined from that point. The damage was done.

At this point I was working with him doing henna tattoos at nightclubs so was earning money. I paid for him to go on a course to learn tattoo make-up etc and we went into a working partnership.

One day at work he was on the phone to one of his ex-girlfriends who had had a termination. She told him how much it would cost and where to go.

"You're going to get rid of it," he told me. "I am not going to stand by you. You have this kid and you are on your own."

I was four months pregnant and in a mess.

He booked me in at a place in Birmingham and we stayed in a hotel the night before the termination.

My belly was so big that we both cried that night.

We were both a mess. We were both very badly damaged as kids and we were worse the older we got, so we never stood a chance together.

# The F Word

Now I don't mean the swear word or the Gordon Ramsay show – but F for freak.

The media started naming people who aren't the norm 'freak' years ago.

But this goes back as far as Victorian days when you could visit the freak show at the travelling circus – see the bearded lady, disfigured people, very overweight people and those born with body defects.

To label somebody a freak because they are born differently to the norm is so degrading for those individuals. And people wonder why society is as it is today.

Perhaps if the media would give these people more respect than the nation would jump on board and follow suit.

You're called a freak for being tattooed, thin, fat, gay, transgender, having surgery – even for being a 'goth'.

So what gives people the right to label you?

And what is the norm nowadays then – because as far as I can see most people today seem to fall into the so-called 'freak' category?

It looks as if the 'normal' folk are the minority. So doesn't that make THEM the freaks of this world? It seems they are the ones not fitting into the lovely society we live in today.

Just because some people are born differently or choose to live THEIR LIVES in a different way, this does not give anyone the right to make a false judgement does it?

Life is hard enough without being put in a box and labelled.

We are all human beings with feelings and a heart. Because someone lives a little bit differently does not give anybody the right to degrade them.

# Daniel and beyond

I really did not want to get rid of my son. I had a scan so I knew the baby was a boy. I named him Daniel.

If only I had been stronger, but I was too weak and on the brink of suicide. And I had H to consider. And I was doing my best to bring him up.

On the morning of the termination I had to be weighed and have my blood pressure taken.

Mr Blond came in with me to see the doctor.

"Has anyone ever died through having a termination?" he asked the doctor.

"No," he replied.

And I swear on my life, within minutes of him saying 'no' the alarm went off to call the doctor.

A woman had just died.

There were loads of us waiting for a termination, even girls of 12 and 13 years old with their parents. I sat there for hours on my own and could not stop crying. I held the coffee cup and got scalded on my hand because I was shaking so much. Meanwhile Mr Blond went off to phone one of his girlfriends.

Eventually the nurses came out and said all terminations were cancelled for that day because of what had happened. I had tried to mentally psyche myself up to basically murder my child – then it was cancelled.

We drove, me crying all the way. Mr Blond had gone quite quiet.

It was as if God was telling me 'this has happened for a reason'.

Back home I waited another week and a half, then got a letter to go to another clinic, so by this time I was just under 20 weeks pregnant.

I think at that point if I had not had H I would have jumped out of the car on my way and killed myself because I was in such a bad place. If I had killed myself at least I would have gone with my son.

Mr Blond drove me there again. This time he said: "If you don't want to do it, don't do it. But I am not going to leave this girl." So he did give me the choice. I cried all the way there and just held my stomach.

We went to this big white house where there was the same sort of smell as the other place. I was sick before I went into the big waiting room with the other women. I could hear the women crying and there was a smell of death, horrible. I have never ever smelt that before.

All I could think of was this baby would not be born healthy because by this time I was addicted to painkillers, taking about 60 odd a day. I started taking them for physical pain, but they made me numb, stopped my brain working, giving me blurred vision and an empty feeling like a robot. And I was drinking vodka, Southern comfort and Jack Daniels.

All this was in my head when a really kind nurse came to get me. She was trying to make me OK. She was being really happy and she hugged me.

I sat on my bed, had the curtain pulled round and put a gown on. I would not stop cradling my stomach, holding Daniel.

It was like a cattle market. I had to walk to the operating room where I could see another woman. There were other people hurting just as much. I saw the woman and they pulled the curtain across.

Because I was so far gone I had to give birth to Daniel. They inject the baby so it is stillborn. My baby had gone to Jesus when he was born. I was given the option to hold him but I didn't.

The experience was to be a turning point in my life.

I just did not want to breathe any more, did not want to be alive any more. Going through that – knowing I could be so evil.

Even as I write this I cannot stop the tears. How could I live with myself? I took someone's life. I took my baby's life. I killed my son – and I can't ever change that.

When I came out the staff gave me a cup of tea and slice of toast. Then the nurse just left me because I was trying to go to sleep. I could hear a woman crying, but no one speaking, it was horrible.

I remember this child came in, about 14 years old. She was on her own and she was breaking her heart. But I couldn't cuddle her. I was no mum – I just sat and watched her cry.

If people only knew the real consequences of unprotected sex.

We didn't speak all the way home after I had taken my baby away. I couldn't even breathe properly because I couldn't stop crying.

There's a song by Puff Daddy which he sings about his friend being killed – Every Breath You Take. The words are so poignant – about being in heaven and waiting for me at the gates.

I felt as if I had lost everything and as if my heart had been turned black. This completely changed me as a person, making me hard, even to this day.

Mr Blond dropped me off – then went to spend the night with his girlfriend. She knew about the baby and later took great pleasure in telling me he fucked her that night.

Mum knew about the termination and was looking after H.

So I went home on my own.

That night I had had it. As stupid as this sounds I knew H was better off without me because I was such an awful person.

I took an overdose of painkillers and drank so much. The only way I could stop this hurt inside was to stop breathing.

I was lying on the sofa in my white fluffy dressing gown – when I swear Gang Gang shook me to wake me. Then he pulled me up by the collar of my dressing gown. People will say 'what a load of bollocks' but I know what I felt and saw. He stood in front of me, pulled my hood and jolted me upright. He just stood there – he was there – as if he had not died.

Then I was so sick.

Mum looked after H so I did not see him for a few days.

Mr Blond accused me of being a drama queen and trying to trap him, trying to make him feel bad. I never saw him in the same light again.

After Daniel I was in limbo. I loved H but I was a bad mum, just distant from him. He was still a baby and I loved him, but I was taking so many painkillers that I got used to feeling numb, it was an everyday occurrence. I knew I had to look after H, but did not know what I was doing and felt so alone. I knew by taking the painkillers it would stop the pain, but it wouldn't stop me being a mum. After all H didn't have a dad so I had to keep going for him.

After a while Mr Blond became apologetic and we started to see each other again. I gradually built myself up again hour by hour, day by day. I got to a semi human state – still really black and cold inside, but breathing. I had no feeling beyond anything I did. Whatever I had to do I just did, with no feeling, no emotion. I had cried more tears than I had water in my body. For about a year I went through the motions of living.

But I had fallen back in love with Mr Blond. He was still with this woman and said he could not end it. I had no self respect; I did not want to be with anyone else so I put up with it.

# Father and Daughter

This is so very hard for me to write as it hurts so much.

All I ever wanted was to be 'daddy's little girl' and even now at the age of 38 it's very difficult to write without crying.

But I guess time doesn't heal in some cases.

You can have the pain of broken bones or go through the most horrific incidents, but nothing hurts as much as not having your father's love. When I was little, yes I know, I was bought gifts and pets to keep me quiet. But it's so hard never having love as you grow up – and this does shape you into the person you become as an adult.

My dad wasn't hard on me and my brother Darryl, but he was quite strict so we would know our place if you understand. We would not be allowed in the kitchen on Sunday afternoons after dinner because dad would be asleep on the floor in front of the fire. We were not allowed to speak when the news or the pools results were on – and God help us if we did. We also had to help around the house and garden, which I loved because I was spending time with my mum in the house or dad in the garden. I'm sure, whether you're a boy or girl (but especially a little girl) you want your mum and dad (especially dad) to be proud of you.

At the time I couldn't understand why I hated my reflection. I would sit for ages looking at this person staring back into my own eyes and ask 'Who am I? Why am I me? Why do I have to look like this? Why is my nose so big? Why are my ears a funny shape? Why am I bony?' I would ask myself these questions time after time.

Then I would say to myself 'Dad doesn't love you because you're ugly'.

Even when I was little I would call myself 'It' – because to me I was never a person.

I used to just sit and cry looking at 'It' looking back at me. So I stopped looking in mirrors for a while from a very young age – hoping that I would have changed the next time I did look. My Aunty Ivy read me The Ugly Duckling when I was a kiddie. So that's what I wanted to be – a beautiful white swan, not some grey ugly little duckling that no one loved or wanted.

I wanted to tell my mum and dad how I felt and ask them if it was just part of growing up. Was the way I was feeling what every boy and girl went through? But I never could ask as I didn't know how to talk to mum and dad and I was too scared of rejection.

I would take my mum's make-up and put so much of it on that my face was covered. Then I would pull my long hair over it – then get yelled at and made to scrub it off.

When dad was a home I would just sit and watch him and long for him to tell me he loved me and that I was beautiful and his little princess – but that day never came.

When parents' evenings were held at school dad never said 'I'm proud of you' or even 'well done' for being good at gymnastics.

I have a really vivid memory of when I was about 16 and I had got really big. I had put on a lot of weight to hide behind, to cover the 'It' creature. I remember my dad saying: "I can't believe just how FAT you are. Look at your legs, your stomach – you're FAT."

Well dad, that messed me up so much. You hurt me more than you will ever know saying those things to me.

I have another memory of when I started my periods at a very, very early age. I remember my dad saying to my mum at the top of his voice: "That's it now. We'll have to watch her now. I'm not having her getting up the duff."

Oh my God. I was a little girl – and my dad thought so little of me? He thought so low of me that I would have had sex at that age? How could he? What did he think I had done that was so wrong that he could say those things?

I worked so hard as a teenager. I bought my own house at the age of 18. I have always worked, given him a beautiful little grandson, tried to make a good life for my son and me – but no, I never heard 'I'm proud of you'.

So dad – I'm sorry you could never be proud of me or love me for being me. But I do love you and always will, even though you have broken contact with me and told me I'm nothing to you any more when I tried to say I was sorry (for something I hadn't done) just so you would speak to me again.

But no, you wouldn't. You just told me I am no daughter of yours.

Well you're still my daddy and I'm sorry I am a disappointment to you.

I love you dad.

# Despair

Still with Mr Blond and still in pain.

Oh I could cope with physical pain it was what he did to me inside. He split my heart in two and made me stop trusting people. He used to cheat on me constantly, belittle me, call me names, then be violent.

I would say to him that I would tell his girlfriend we were still seeing each other. With one breath he wanted to be with me.

"Well I'll tell her," I'd say. "Don't you think she has a right to know?"

I never saw Mr Blond out of malice to her – to me he was my man, the man I loved and did not want to lose. But he knew I had no self respect. I had BDD, yet he would always make reference to other women, commenting on the size of their tits for example or saying: "I have had her" and all crap like that.

Even when he was with me he would look at other women constantly. His phone would always go off and he would be sneaking off to the toilet to answer it – which all made me feel even more worthless.

Around this time I had gone for a routine cancer smear and it showed that I had 'abnormal' cells. Stupidly I ignored the warning.

When I was called back for another test I was told I had cervical cancer.

I just thought it was karma for what I had done to Daniel.

I had to go through chemotherapy which made me so ill that I could not even stand up, walk, talk or move. I even smelt different and looked like a corpse. My hair, which was blonde and beautifully, naturally curly, was falling out in clumps. Even the hair from my eyelashes and eyebrows fell out. I was so ill I had to stay at mum's.

Mr Blond just fucked off to Miami at a time when I was so ill I could have died.

Gradually I recovered and was lucky enough to go into remission.

But he continued cheating on me and took great pleasure in telling me I had no proof. But I would find an earring, a false finger nail, jewellery or make-up at his place.

Once I went under the bed to get my shoes and there was a pair of women's pants. These were size 14 from M&S and they had been worn if you know what I mean, let's just say 'crusty old cottage cheese', then you will. When I threw them at him he said he had found them on the street and brought them home as a souvenir. He said I was making a mountain out of a mole hill as usual.

He would phone me when he was with one of his whores accidentally on purpose so I could hear him on the other end of the phone. So after listening to his conversations time after time with these women I would sit on the floor, crying uncontrollably, wanting him so much, wanting him to come and take the pain away – but he never did. I would be rocking backward and forward, a mess. I wanted him to see what he had done to me, but he didn't care anyway.

There was a girl who lived in the same block of flats as him. She was a singer, a pretty blonde, skinny and looked like Debbie Harry.

We had gone out one night to a few bars and Mr Blond sang with her on the karaoke. I was jealous, but didn't say anything. Then we all went back to her flat where I sat on the sofa, he sat on a chair – and she sat on his knee, wearing a skimpy outfit. He was cuddling and kissing her in front of me. She said something about his dad and he told her he had passed away then started crying so she was comforting him. I just sat there like a twat while he told her: "I will always love you. If I am still on my own when I am 50 I will marry you."

He said it in front of me!

Yet he would never even walk with me or hold my hand.

And she loved it because she had got one up on me. I felt such a worthless piece of shit.

Once we had a weekend in Blackpool and his phone was in his pocket when it 'accidentally' phoned some girl (he blamed me that the phone rang her). She heard us talking – and until then she thought she was his only girl. He only realised when she rang him back later – and he was furious.

Just before we went to Blackpool I had had a tummy tuck.

But when he realised the girl had heard us he started banging on the door of our hotel room we had argued about something or other and I had gone back to the room alone. I was so frightened I wet myself because I knew what he was capable of doing and what he was going to do to me. He came bursting into our room, picked me up by the throat and chucked me on the bed. When I got up off the bed he kicked me in the stomach and I fell onto the floor. He used to wear big boots so the blow burst my stomach open.

Then he just left me. The hotel called the police because of the commotion but I didn't press any charges.

My next plastic surgery was a nose job and it worked beautifully. I had a really lovely nose.

But I was back with Mr Blond. We went out one night and this girl kept coming up to him and he was really sheepish with me and pushed me aside. He got really drunk and when we went home his phone kept ringing in his jeans pocket. By the time he passed out on the bed he had about 30 missed calls. Then it rang again and the name 'Dave' came up on the phone so I answered it – but it was her.

By this time I had been with Mr Blond for years, but she told me she had been fucking him for six months and that she was his girlfriend. I actually knew this girl and I knew it was someone he had shagged years before. I felt as if she had a hold on me, as if she could have my boyfriend whenever she wanted.

I was so mad and upset I slapped him full in the face while he was asleep.

He woke immediately in an absolute rage, grabbing me and slamming me into the wall. I fled into the hallway where he had a telephone on the wall and I tried to phone the police. But he punched me in the back of the head, started kicking me on the floor, then grabbed the handset off me and smashed it straight into my face.

My nose was gone... my beautiful nose... I had only had it for a few months!

After that incident he ran off, but not before going to the car park and scratching my car all over.

When Mr Blond flips he is really evil and God help whoever is in his way.

The police were involved in the incident where he smashed my nose, but even after that I was frightened of losing him so I dropped the charges. In fact I have dropped charges against Mr Black and Mr Blond.

Mr Black used to say to me that if I went to the police it would be the biggest mistake of my life.

But with Mr Blond he could easily have murdered me ten times over.

I remember one particular occasion when we were working at the tattoo shop. This girl, who I knew he fancied, came in and was really bolshy, completely ignoring me. She went straight past me and into the treatment room and demanded Mr Blond gave her a tattoo. She started shouting so I told him to get her out.

He went out and came back about two hours later. I was on the phone at the time. He calmly shut the shop door then put the phone receiver down to cut me off.

He wrapped the telephone cord around my throat, then lifted me up by my throat until I passed out, then left me.

But we would always get back together and of course things would get worse.

I was starting to get over Daniel, though still feeling raw.

But when H was about four Mr Black was back on the scene. Our divorce had been finalised and he was being really threatening towards me.

By this time I had suffered three miscarriages with Mr Blond, my BDD was really bad and I was at an all time low, very depressed.

And I was pregnant by him again. Worse still, as soon as I was pregnant I knew there was something wrong. This time it felt completely different.

Mr Blond was still with his woman and denied the baby was his yet again. Good at that aren't they? He had been with her by now for about 12 years.

Although I was weak and emotional I felt as if I was strong enough to look after kids, so I was not going to abort again.

But Mr Blond was about to push me over the edge. He had gone out with the lads in the band – and they had taken some girls with them. I knew he had done stuff with one of the girls so my heart was aching. I rang him but he would not answer the phone. I needed to talk to him because I knew he was with someone else.

I was in bed when he accidentally on purpose rang me so I could hear what they were saying – just to hurt me. I listened for about half an hour to 45 minutes as they were laughing and joking. He used to do that all the time to me.

I heard him say to her: "Come over here sexy and give me that blow job you promised me earlier."

Then the phone went dead…

I was physically sick; I actually projectile vomited and lay in bed covered in sick. I cried so much that I thought my brain would stop working. I hurt so much – even on the inside of my face, inside my skull, my eyes. I thought I would die from the pain because my head hurt so much. I have never felt such emptiness in ages.

And there was the realisation – I had let Daniel die for this man – a man who was a worthless piece of shit, someone who had taken my happiness away from me.

I kept ringing him but got no answer, just voicemail.

Two hours later he 'accidentally' rang (whatever!), so I could hear them in bed. I will leave it to your imagination what they were doing. I threw my phone up the wall. I had had it.

I phoned my neighbour at about 1am and just cried. She listened then told me to get some sleep.

I went into H's room and watched him sleeping. As I looked at him it was as if a light bulb came on in my head. I thought 'if you bring him up he will be a wreck like you'.

I thought I could not inflict me on him anymore. I didn't want that for my son.

Although he would hurt if I died he would get over it.

So I took pills and drank.

I don't know how she knew but my neighbour came round at 4am and found me unconscious on the kitchen floor. She called an ambulance and went to hospital with me while her husband looked after H.

I had a stomach pump, tubes down my throat and up my nose, and was put on a drip.

What a reality check – the guilt I felt when I came round. And I still carry that with me today, that I was so selfish. Even though I was a shit human being I was going to take that away from my son who had done no harm to anybody. I was so selfish to have even thought about doing that to my baby. It made me realise that it doesn't matter how much someone hurts me, H is always going to love me. I will always have the love of my son and no man will ever come close to that. I have something in my life I never dreamed of – the love I have from H, the love I always wanted and craved for, is 1,000 times more than for any man.

I began working in a massive 'adult shop' – a sex shop. One day at work I started to feel really ill again, this time with terrible stomach cramps.

Mr Blond was performing with his band in a concert that night and for some reason he wanted me to go with him. I don't know why because he usually completely ignored me. Anyway, although I didn't feel well I went. As the band played I was in agony. The bass was so loud it was vibrating my body. Eventually I told a friend of his that I felt really ill and he took me home.

H was at my neighbours; there was just me and Reggie the dog at home. So I got a hot water bottle, made myself a drink and went to bed.

By 3am I was in absolute agony and went downstairs to the kitchen to make a cup of tea. I had just the worst pain; it felt as if something was ripping my insides out. Then I felt wet and realised I was losing blood.

I phoned mum and she came round, still wearing her nightie and slippers.

I sat on the kitchen floor because I was in so much pain that I couldn't move. I could hear Reggie lapping something. I put the light on and Reggie was licking up the baby.

I was about 10 weeks gone and had miscarried on the kitchen floor.

That freaked me out; it was horrible; I was a wreck.

I am very fertile, but not strong enough to carry a child.

And looking back I don't think the baby, who I named Amelia Rose (Millie), could have survived. I was 34 years old, drinking heavily, addicted to painkillers and taking coke. I did ring him again, but yet again he ignored my call.

But that was it. Done. From that moment I stopped having sex with Mr Blond. He had killed any craving I had to be loved, the craving that I had all my life – and I resent him for that to this day (but there will always be a part of me that will love him as well).

I am not blaming Mr Blond for anything. What happened happened. I am not holding grudges. He did what he did and nothing can change that. I know he is not a strong person so I don't blame him. He does have a good heart, but he was not for me. When someone breaks down his brick wall you will find a good man inside because he can be loving and caring. A lot of his problems were down to drink, drugs and insecurity.

But all this has made me a stronger person now – colder – but stronger.

# Dysmorphia in Your 30s

When I was in my late teens/early 20s all I could think of was 'oh well, when I'm older this self-loathing will go and I can just live a so-called normal life'.

I thought I would not be consumed with all this hatred for myself, would not be constantly crying, and would not be performing the make-up on/make-up off routine day after day.

But unfortunately for me it just got worse.

Instead I had the pressures of gaining weight, losing weight, changing body shape – and getting wrinkles.

I can remember getting my first line (OK 'wrinkle') as if it was yesterday.

Oh how bloody fantastic. So not only am I fat with a face like the Wicked Witch of the West from the Wizard of Sodding Oz I now have bleeding wrinkles. This just gets better and better…

I really did think that when I got older my dysmorphia might ease a bit, but now I'm dealing with a whole new ball game – from wrinkles to bingo wings (saggy skin under the arms), an ass down to me knees, thread veins, droopy eyelid syndrome, turkey woggle neck – and (this is a beauty just to piss me off even more) varicose veins. Oh my God. And I wonder why I am single.

So now comes the 'buy cream for this/buy cream for that' stage of my life. I think my bathroom and bedroom contain more of these stupid miracle cures than sodding Boots. And the money I have spent on cellulite cream is just a joke.

My legs, ass and bingo wings were made to store the devil's dimples.

And before anyone says 'a healthy diet and eating right will get rid of cellulite' – then think again, 'cause trust me, there's no hope.

No matter how much I exercised, how well I ate, or verged on anorexia it still did not go. If I gained weight it was like the plague covering my body. Even my back had it. When I lost weight did it go? Er – no. Did it buggery. It lingered like a bad smell. But this time it was accompanied by saggy skin and silver stretch marks. Now my body was being taken over by a stampeding herd of cowing silver fish. Now they're ugly. My stretch marks are so big you could quite securely park your bike in 'em. They're like crepe paper, all thin to the touch, but dead wrinkly. And the fat deposits around them just makes them stand out even bleeding more 'cos you get fat lumpy bumpy bits at the beginning and end of your stretch marks.

Crikey, I'm painting a beautiful picture of myself aren't I?

And there's no part of my body where a stretchy hasn't targeted itself. I have them all over, even on the back of me knees for the love of God. My legs look like a deflated lilo from the back. My poor inner ankles are being taken over by bright purple red thread veins; me ankles are like a map of Britain. Now if I just shove a satellite dish up me ass I'd be a sodding sat nav with these legs.

Now I don't know if it's just me or when ladies get to a certain age (and yes I'm calling myself a lady 'cos no one else will), but the backs of me thighs are sprouting thick, black, curly hairs. I don't know if this is normal, but I highly doubt it. I didn't even notice I had them 'till my little boy H said: "Mum, you've got something crawling up your leg."

He pulled it and I nearly hit the roof 'cos they were still attached to me leg.

Now by body looks like it's made from play dough – all squishy and squashy. I dread to think what I am going to look like in 5 years if I look this bad now. I'd sooner pull me brains out of me nose with a rusty nail then ever be naked in front of a man again. So I'm going to stay under me rock where I belong until it's time for Jesus for me. Yeah, I'm gonna be a miserable old spinster on me own.

# Reggie

I must devote a chapter to Reggie, my Staffie.

Ever since I was a little girl I always wanted a pure blood Irish white Staffie.

As I have said we had Reggie because H was a mess after his dad left, very withdrawn and regressed. He had gone from a bubbly little kid to chewing his lips until they bled. I tried my hardest to help him but he wouldn't talk, he would shake and wee the bed.

It was Mr Blond who suggested we should get him a dog and he found someone who was selling Staffies. We went to see a group of about six little Irish Staffie pups. They were lovely, but I didn't knit with any of them.

Then the door bashed open and this fat puppy with a big pink belly came sliding through on his arse. It was like something out of a Walt Disney film. He ran round the corner, ran into the fire surround and smashed ornaments and then sat there bemused.

"That's him," I said. "That's the one that I want."

I later took H to see the pups and asked him which one he liked – and he picked Reggie straight away. He would pick Reggie up and let him sleep in the arm of his coat; he was just the friendliest dog.

Reggie would make the most awful noise, screaming at the top of his voice if you left him at the bottom of the stairs, so H took him to bed with him. Reggie would later jump out of H's bed the scramble up the underside of my quilt and sleep on my pillow with me. Then H would join us some time in the morning. They were inseparable.

And H grew in confidence. He would play with Reggie and talk to him constantly. Reggie came everywhere with us. He ate his meals with us, would sit on our knee, he eventually became a brilliant, well behaved dog, the best dog in the world.

But to start with he was boisterous and would chew stuff when he was teething badly.

One day I was at work and H was at school. When I came home I thought I had been burgled. Reggie had pissed and shit all over the house. He had been in the plant pots, chewed the yucca plants to bits, wrecked the sofa, chewed the kitchen cupboards and carpets – even pissed and shit all over me bed. He was a bugger; and I had only left him for three hours.

So I went to the pet shop and bought him a puppy cage which he loved. And H used to sit inside it with him!

By the time Reggie was six months old he was massive and sturdy with a bone structure that was out of this world. His head was more like that of a two-year old. Reggie was a freak of nature, with a square head at just a few months old.

If I had a fall out with Mr Blond or found out he was with yet another woman I would sit at the top of the stairs and talk to Reggie while in floods of tears and he would put his paw on my arm, or leg. Even if Reggie was fast asleep if he heard me crying he would come up to me.

If we went out in the car Reggie would sit in the seat and 'sing' to the song *Dilemma* by Nelly and Kelly. He would tap his paw on my shoulder and stick his head out of the sunroof.

Reggie had his own T shirt and bandana and would sleep in his own jimjams. As soon as he saw his jimjams he would just sit there waiting to be dressed, knowing it was time for bed.

Reggie had his own proper wardrobe in H's room, including his own pants. He hated his tail and would chew it so badly I thought he might have to have it amputated. He would knock into stuff chasing his tail.

But he loved water. As soon as I turned the tap on in the bathroom he was there and would even jump in the bath with me.

When it was H's birthday Reggie would have his party hat on. He was not like a dog; he was everything to us.

When I was at home with him and H was due home I'd say: "Who's coming?" He would look at me then sit at the front door squealing; or he would sit at the top of the road waiting for H.

We would take Reggie to the park and he never needed to have his lead on.

I saved up for ages and managed to book a caravan in Mable Thorpe so we took Reggie with us. The caravan was near the beach so I told H to take Reggie for a walk. Soon H came screaming back saying: "Reggie is dead."

But he had just found a massive hole in the sand where he dragged a huge pile of seaweed in and fell asleep under it! I had to jump into the hole to get him out. So after that we put him on a harness to run up and down the beach.

Reggie loved seafood – and just like a kid he would eat toffee apples and candyfloss at the local 'goose fair'.

And he was such a good guard dog.

One November, when me and Mr Blond were going through a hard patch, I was at home putting up the Christmas decorations, yeah, in November, so what? We loved Crimbo time. He had cheated on me again and had been found out (with a girl he said he had stopped seeing years ago) but he denied it. I knew he was bullshitting because she told me.

It was a Sunday night and I was playing Christmas carols on the CD player. H was upstairs and it was our usual routine. H, who was about six at the time, would have a bath then sit upstairs on his bed watching TV with Reggie.

While I was struggling to get the Christmas tree out I had told H to go upstairs to watch the telly and eat his tea until I got the tree out so he could then help me decorate it.

Then there was a bang on the door – a real bang – as if the bailiffs were at the door. But I could see it was Mr Blond. I opened the door and he was going nuts – reckoned I was seeing someone else (I wasn't). He pushed me over and I bashed my head at the bottom of the stairs. I had this massive, heavy gargoyle of a Staffie (which was supposed to ward off the evil spirits) on a big plinth. It was about 4ft tall, a present for my 30th birthday, and I loved it. He pushed it over and smashed it in temper because he knew I loved it. While I was trying to shield H from all this Mr Blond was calling me all the names under the sun, yet I had done nothing wrong. Because he had been caught out he needed to turn the tables so it was my fault. But I had never cheated on him, never looked at another bloke.

Mr Blond left the house, then came back in again, slammed the door and went.

H tried to help me lift the gargoyle then I sat on the stairs crying.

I presumed Reggie was frightened and had run upstairs, but I knew in my heart what had happened.

"Go and check on Reggie," I told H so he went upstairs.

"He's not here," he shouted down – and just then there was a bang on the door – and I knew.

I opened the door and Mr Blond stood there.

"Where's my boy (Reggie)? What have you done to him?" I said.

"I didn't mean to do it," came the reply.

I pushed him over into the bushes and ran past him.

It was pouring down with rain and I only had a silky bath robe on but I ran down the road. My friend, the next door neighbour, heard the commotion and came round as I was running up the street. She looked after H, but I could hear him screaming for Reggie.

I saw a bus at the top of the road and all these people there.

Reggie, who was still only 18 months old, was lying in the road with his head on the pavement. I was screaming. I just sat on the pavement and put his head on my lap. He looked at me and blood came out of his mouth.

Reggie died in my arms.

I tried to carry him but he weighed about six stones. All these people were trying to help me and I was covered in blood, but all I could do was scream at them.

The guy from next door came out with a cardboard box and me and Mr Blond put Reggie in my car.

My neighbours followed me in their car to mum's with H in their car as I did not want him in my car with Reggie's body. H didn't know Reggie was dead at this point; he just thought he was poorly. I took Reggie to my mum's where I stayed with him all night, cradling him, giving him drops of water. I couldn't believe he was dead because he was still warm. When I lifted him onto me his body was soft. His back and his ribcage had been broken. My boy had left us forever.

The next morning it was still raining.

We dug a hole under the apple tree at mum's and buried my little baby boy Reggie with his favourite treats in the world: his musical Christmas antlers which he always loved, a pig's ear, a bar of Dairy Milk (which was his favourite chocolate), his squeaky pink bunny, his comfort blanket which he took everywhere with him like a child does, and his T shirt.

That dog meant more to me and H than anyone could imagine. He helped me and H through such a bad stage in our lives and I don't know what H would have turned into without him.

But now H was a wreck again and could not stop crying; back to chewing his lips and making them bleed, weeing his pants and not speaking.

I believe to this day Mr Blond encouraged Reggie to come out and cross the road knowing it would hurt me.

Reggie had been hit by a car before because he was able to jump the 6ft double gate or hurl himself over it.

The first time he was hit I heard the screech of brakes then a bump. The woman driver was hysterical. But Reggie just got up

– and did that twice more. The last time he did that a woman driver slowed down and swerved because a cat ran out; and she hit Reggie on the pavement. Reggie was actually lying under the tyre, but got up and shook himself.

After Reggie's death because of the way H was I thought I had better get another dog quickly.

I rang the Staffie Protection and told them that if they had a white Staffie come in to let me know. As soon as I put the receiver down the phone rang.

"We've just had one brought in," the lady said. "But he is in a bit of a mess. You can't look now because we don't know if it will survive. It's petrified and really timid."

I went straight over.

It was raining again, it always seemed to be raining after Reggie died, and the woman showed me to the dog pen. The kennel maids were trying to get him out of the wind and rain but he would not go near them. I sat with him for a couple of hours. We were both absolutely wet through and frozen because the wind was so bad.

He was only a puppy and had been used as bait in a dog fight so they would get a taste for blood. The RSPCA had been involved and the two dogs had had to be destroyed.

His face was ripped to bits, his tail was broken, his jowls were ripped open, his claws ripped out, something had been squirted in his eyes, he had been marked with spray paint and he stank.

Then he came to me.

I took him to the emergency vet myself and he was in there for about a week.

As soon as H saw him he burst into tears.

Ronnie is now eight years old and weighs 12 stone – and he and H are inseparable.

Three years ago I asked H if we should have another dog. One of my friends had pups and no one wanted the runt of the litter. They brought him to us on the back of a motorbike travelling down the motorway in a rucksack on the bloke's back!

When we first saw 'Diddy Poo' I thought 'that's the ugliest thing I have ever seen in my life!'

Because of what he went through, Ronnie does not like other dogs, but gets on fine with Diddy Poo.

We have been a little family ever since.

# A Nobody

I was a nobody – a single mum. I had nothing at the time. I was reduced to scrimping in H's money pot for 2ps and 1ps to buy food. I couldn't pay bills and my debts were getting so high that there was interest being added on to interest making my debts even greater, and I had constant letters from the bank about my overdraft.

There seemed no end to it. I had no money and I had to find £1,000 or the bailiffs were coming to take stuff away – which would have included things belonging to H such as his telly and video. H had already lost his dad and was going to lose his home so I couldn't let that happen.

The bailiffs told me if I paid £500 within a few days this would stop them coming, so I borrowed £50 off mum (she couldn't afford anymore) and sold jewellery, but I still couldn't find the rest of the money.

I had massive debts left by my ex-husband and my poxy Ford Fiesta that I was still having to pay off that was worth about £100.

Out of respect for H I do not want to go into great detail about what happened next. But suffice to say I was working in a sex shop and was offered the chance to earn some money by appearing in a movie in Bristol.

When I arrived in Bristol, having scraped together my last money for the train fare, which I was getting back he said, the film director told me the movie was more explicit than I had been told and he had some requests of his own he wanted complied with first.

Unless I did as I was asked I would just get the train home – without the money I so badly needed to keep the bailiffs away.

I was taking many painkillers at the time, still trying to keep myself feeling numb from my problems. The painkillers worked for me – taking away every ounce of emotion as well as every ache and pain. I was addicted, but saw no wrong in what I was doing. What an idiot I was. I had already taken over 20 pills and drank a bottle of wine on the train. I had another bottle of wine when I arrived in Bristol and was crying on the inside. I was only hurting myself while I was in that film studio and really felt like slitting my wrists.

Still hating my body I refused to take my clothes off while I went through the motions trying not to cry thinking 'what the fuck am I doing to myself?'

I hated myself so much and had no respect. I cried all the way home.

There have been similar offers since Big Brother but I would never go there again. It's OK for some people; in fact I have good friends involved in the business, but it's not for me.

I received £300 – which stopped the bailiffs from calling. But no amount of money could ever restore my shame, I hate myself for doing that.

# Plastic Surgery

My life started to change after my plastic surgery, especially after I had my boobs done.

I was 27 at the time.

I decided I wanted to have the biggest breast implants in the UK one day.

After having my third boob job there was a call from the surgeon's public relations agents asking if I would be prepared to do a newspaper article about my boobs.

I agreed to that. Then I took part in a TV documentary which was looking at the reasons women had their boobs done.

From there it just escalated.

Newspapers were getting in touch with me asking me to do glamour work. I would also be a guest on chat shows and do some modelling, working at road shows and stints as a 'pit stop girl'. I started to get requests for interviews and photo shoots for magazines interested in the whole surgery thing.

I was glad to be doing all this because, even though I had always longed to be an actress, at least this was in the industry I had craved to be in since I was a little girl. This was a huge thing for me – doing what I had always wanted to do 30 years after dreaming of being an actress. I was finally in show business, well, a little bit anyway – and now I looked nothing like I used to. And I started to feel differently about myself.

This was really nice for me. That horrible panicky feeling I used to get as soon as I woke up was slipping away, because I knew when I woke up that I looked different. Even though I was not 100 per cent how I wanted to look, it was more like I wanted to be.

I started my surgery in 1997 – my boobs first.

I had gone from 24 stones to five stones and four pounds. I had the confidence from losing the weight – but I had gained the skin. So I was happier being thin, but miserable with the excess skin!

Before I had surgery to move excess skin I could actually pick my stomach up, lift it up and hold it out in front of me with my arms stretched.

My inspiration of course was Pamela Anderson from Baywatch who was massive at the time (in more ways than one).

I just thought: 'I can change the way I look,' so I made some enquiries. And if I was going to have breast implants I thought I might as well have the biggest – but this had to be done gradually as you have to find out the elasticity of your skin. I had set a goal for myself and this was really what I wanted. I just like big boobs – so I went to Transform in Nottingham.

After my first boob job I went from a 30AAA to a 30E. It was better, but I was not happy. As far as I was concerned they weren't big enough.

"Is that it?" I thought. Clearly I was not over the moon.

After I lost everything from my break up with Mr Black and thought I had paid off all the debts, there was some equity left from the house and a good friend, who was financially secure, helped pay off the debts in the end, so that's what I used for my 'real' surgery. But there were other debts he had run up in joint names which I wasn't aware of until later. (That's when I had to take part in 'the film').

So, thinking I was fine for money, I had my second boob job – then had my teeth done. My teeth were really corroded from all the acid due to throwing up, so the dentist filed my teeth down until they were just stubs, then connected veneer onto eight of them. That was one of the most painful things I have had done.

But it had to be done. I was so paranoid about my black, awful teeth I could not smile. There are a lot of down sides to having an eating disorder and that is one of them.

Then I had a nose job as it had been broken (again).

Then I had my boobs done again. I have had five boob op's in total between 1997 and 2005. But I still want them bigger... and I will.

They are a size 30M now and I would like them another six cups bigger. I will be having more surgery, even though there were problems after my third one. The muscle was contracting around the implants, trying to reject them (which is called encapsulation), so it was really painful.

So shortly after that I paid for 'designer implants' which were much better, though the first ones to arrive were too small.

I have invested a lot of money in 'me'.

I had my boobs, a tummy tuck and liposuction all done at the same time.

I remember crying because to me my boobs looked no different.

And I suffered from gangrene as a result of the tummy tuck. I told the surgeons I wanted a really flat tummy, so they had to remove so much skin that they made me sign a special consent form first in case there were problems.

You have to wear this corset thing around your waist and because I had had so much skin removed my stomach was rock hard; you could not even pinch a millimetre of skin.

I felt my stomach go 'pop' and I could see it was bleeding; then it started weeping but I thought 'It'll be alright'. I was petrified to move because I thought my stomach would rip open. I had to keep the corset on during a red hot summer and the smell from the wound was horrendous, like rotting flesh. It was becoming so bad that bluebottles were being attracted into the house. The smell was repulsive.

The wound was stapled together, but two or three of the staples had come out – leaving a gaping hole with a piece of skin over it, flapping open like an envelope.

I went to the clinic and they stapled it to pull the flesh back together and they gave me antibiotics.

But that night I had an epileptic fit.

It took me about eight weeks to recover from the whole experience.

I had liposuction on my legs. God that was awful, horrendous, the worst thing I have had done. Lipo' makes you go lumpy. They fill you up with saline to dilute the fat, then suck it all out; but when the saline starts to ooze out of the holes you are left with lumps of fat. It's the biggest waste of money. But I had it done three times – now I need a thigh lift because they sucked out so much fat there's all this skin left behind. And whatever people say, you can't work that off.

I had to wear surgical stockings and I was in the most agonising pain from my legs. I went back to have more lipo' done – and had my nose done (again) because it had been broken. Then boobs done again, then more lipo'…

All this was being done while I was with Mr Blond – but he couldn't have given a shit. I am still really badly scarred from the operation.

I didn't do it for a man, for work or attention anyway; I did it for me because I didn't like the way I looked. It was to make me feel better about feeling alive. If you don't make yourself happy no one else is going to do it for you.

I know people will always criticise me and accuse me of being superficial. But if you have excess skin then what are you supposed to do about it? Because you get criticised if you would have just left it, so of course, I had it cut off.

And I don't care if people like what they see or not as long as I am happy.

Next I'll be having upper and lower eyelid lifts where they remove excess skin. Then I'll have butt cheek implants, then a mini face lift. I also need my bottom teeth straightened and veneered.

Then I'll have a face lift and neck lift.

Then I'll have my boobs done again.

Some people buy new cars. I buy new body parts.

I think if you want surgery go ahead, as long as you are doing it for you, not for a man or woman or for financial gain – as long as it makes you happy as a person. Don't have surgery for someone else.

For me, surgery is the best feeling in the world because I go in to the operating theatre looking hideous and come out a little less hideous. All the bruising and pain is worth it. And despite everything I don't feel I've suffered that much considering the amount of surgery I've had.

When I look back so many things have stopped me from dying; there have been so many different factors that have brought me through. I feel I am still here for a reason; if I was not meant to be here I would have died years ago.

Without surgery I know I would be a wreck, a recluse – then what would have happened to H and my mum? Dysmorphia is such a huge part of my life that I am glad I had surgery. So if you are 'umming and ahhing' about it, don't ever worry if it will make you happier and more comfortable. Some people do have bad experiences with surgery, but you can't always think of that; sometimes it's nice to think positive. If you're in a positive mental state rather than negative there's more chance of the surgery being 99.9% right.

In this life you can't be defeatist: think positive.

I want to make special mention of the surgeons Dr Aslam from Linia Medical Group from Harley Street in London, Transform Medical Group and Dr Singh from London Bridge. I have nothing but praise for all of them for making me happier with myself than I could have ever been.

# Big Brother

I had watched Big Brother but I was not an avid fan, though I did enjoy it when Jade Goody was in it.

And I thought: "Actually, I would like to do that."

After Big Brother 5 finished there was an advert for Big Brother 6 contestants.

I said to Mr Blond: "I'm going to do that – and I am going to get it."

I absolutely knew I would end up doing it. It was as though my head told me 'you are going to do this' and it felt comfortable.

Mr Blond also wanted to be in it. Ever since I first met him he had been used to being the centre of attention: in fact he would get mad if he wasn't the centre of everything.

So there I was: blonde with big boobs – and people didn't have big boobs in Nottingham then. I still wanted to be famous, just as I had when I was little.

But it was Mr Blond who was famous locally. He was a brilliant guitarist and singer – but never made it big. Yet it's me who made it to a certain level. Although I'm on the bottom rung of the ladder it's still further up than most people.

I went with Mr Blond to that first audition at The Think Tank in Birmingham for Big Brother 6. We got up at 4.30am on a bitterly cold day. It was 2005–06 and Big Brother was massive.

We queued up with everyone – and there were THOUSANDS of people. I thought you had to stand out from the crowd so I wore a white and pink cowgirl outfit. I had a little pink gingham top on with my boobs pushed up like Daisy Duke in The Dukes of Hazard.

So there I was: blonde hair and massive tits. I looked a right twat.

But actually you don't need to stand out from the crowd; you just need to be yourself.

We queued for about five or six hours, Mr Blond telling me not to be disappointed if he got through and I didn't.

"If I get through don't be funny with me," he said.

We had to stand in a line then we were let through in groups of ten or 12.

At the first stage if they like you they stamp your hand with the *Big Brother* eye and you are put through to the next stage. At the second stage they either love you or hate you.

A man from the production company, Endemol, talked to us and stressed you had to impress.

At the second stage they asked me questions and I made them laugh with my funny answers.

"What makes you stand out?" they asked.

"Well, what do you think?" Obviously it's me boobs, being as though "I have the biggest breast implants in Britain," I replied.

Having got through that stage, the next is the 'diary room' where you sit with a black curtain round you and talk to the camera. A disembodied voice asks questions to see what your response is. When I am me I am Lisa – but this was Lea answering. I am in fact constantly acting because I can never be me. The real me is a basket case, miserable, lonely and suffering from BDD.

But Lea says 'fuck it, I can't be arsed'.

The mind is stronger than the body. In my life I have had to learn to live differently from normal people – to manufacture a different 'me' to keep me alive. But sometimes the paths of Lisa and Lea do cross.

Back at the auditions the next stage (Mr Blond did not even get through the first stage!) was to complete a questionnaire – then there was another stint in the diary room.

The next major hurdle was to be called back the next day – and they called me back to Birmingham.

This time there was a games day – team building with others to see how you react with people: whether you are angry, funny, placid or depressed. We had to argue with each other on a subject: one pro, one anti.

Our subject was cosmetic surgery. I was for it!

Next we had to see a lovely psychiatrist.

They phone you if you are in.

I got called back for Big Brother 6!

All I could think was I would not have to worry about money any more.

But the idea of Big Brother is everyone has to be normal and not to have already appeared on TV. And when they found out I had done a TV documentary I was pulled out.

I was gutted. It broke my heart and I thought I would never be considered now.

After losing Big Brother 6 I used to go on websites looking at advertising for TV presenters. I thought I would give that a try.

There was one ad' for a presenter to do with motor sports. Now I love cars, anything with an engine. I got on really well with the guy who told me he owned a production company and was going to make me famous etc. He said he wanted me on the motor sports channel and offered me a lot of money, a huge annual fee and expensive company car. He said he would pay for the photo shoots.

Then he started to come onto me.

"I want you to be with me. I could do this for you," etc.

I had been so gullible. The 'company' was obviously bogus. Diry ode bastard.

Then one day I got a call – a recall for Big Brother 7. So it was back to Birmingham, but again they did not put me through. I was driving home on the motorway when my phone rang.

They had made a mistake they said. I was in and could I go back now?

At this time I was still friends with Mr Blond but not 'with him'.

We were driving to Huntingdon, where I was going to have my nose done, when I told him: "I've got Big Brother you know."

I remember hearing Will Young once say he knew he would be a pop star; he knew he would win The X Factor. He knew in his bones; he knew he would do it.

Everyone who gets Big Brother says the same thing. You know inside you that you have got it. There are no two ways about it. Everybody feels the same.

But the night before I was to leave home I was in tears and phoned Endemol to say I couldn't do it. I just couldn't leave H who was only ten years old and I had never been away from him. How could I leave him? I told him every day that I loved him.

But H came running down the stairs and put the receiver down, then said to me: "If you don't do this you will regret this for the rest of your life. I'll be able to see you every day on the telly! And I'm really proud of you."

(He didn't vote for me though!).

The next morning I got the 6am train to London – and life had changed already. I was travelling first class. First class! Me? I thought this was going to be the best experience of my life. I had never travelled first class before. I didn't even have to pay for the ticket.

"Oh my God I am sitting in first class," was all I could think of.

Before I set off Mr Blond had asked me: "Have you anything to tell me?"

He was trying to say that if I had anything to hide it would come out once I was on Big Brother. But I had never had an affair behind his back.

(I didn't admit to the film. I was not going to admit to something that hadn't even materialised in public).

In London there was a photo session, then a psychiatric test.

I had to stay in a London hotel for the night with my lovely chaperone Eve. I was confined with a chaperone 24 hours a day for two weeks in the run up to Big Brother. Everything was taken away so I did not even have a phone.

I spoke to H at 10am on that April morning – and I was not allowed to speak to him again until the end of July – not a word.

I was a mess, all 'coked up'. I had been getting money for documentaries, clothes shows and various media events: £100 here and there.

The next morning me and Eve got a cab to Waterloo Station, then caught the Eurostar to Belgium. Remember Big Brother was huge at the time – so they took us out of the country. This was the last year when it was such a huge series.

'Precious cargo' they called us. Endemol and Channel 4 were determined to keep us under lock and key despite the fantastic cost of keeping us under wraps.

I was taken to Belgium for two weeks – taken away from my friends and family. During this time contestants are assessed by their chaperone. I was seriously bulimic at the time, so when Eve was asleep I would drink and take pills in the toilet. I didn't eat much, but what I did eat came up.

I had a lovely time in Belgium, but I missed H so much that I said to Eve: "I'm pulling out; I can't do this."

When it gets to this point the chaperone has to phone the Endemol care team who look after families while you are away to make sure the media aren't after them.

The care team Dan and Abi were so brilliant. They reassured Eve that H was OK.

On the second Sunday that we were in Belgium we had come off a boat trip when Eve got a phone call. I remember we were eating chocolate waffles after the boat trip. I was also in a bad mood because I had to wear a disguise that made me look like a bloke: baggy clothes, a brown wig, baseball cap and trainers.

I do not do flats. I was born wearing heels. I will die wearing heels.

Anyway Eve looked at me and I could see she was worried. My first thought was H or my mum, but she said: "Have you made a film?"

"No," I replied.

"Be honest," she said.

Eve said someone had sold a story to the News of the World about a film.

I still denied it because I thought they would pull me out – though I admitted it to her later that night.

It seemed the porn company had waited for this moment to release the film on the Internet and on DVD.

I have never watched it to this day. To me it seems as if that was not me anyway; it was just another one of my little fuckin' characters.

Back from Belgium you have to pack and re-pack your suitcase as you are only allowed a few things. There are rigorous checks to see what you are taking in – like being in the army. We were not allowed lip liner, lipstick, lip pencil – nothing that you could write with. No books, magazines or Ipod.

Sharon and Phil from Endemol talked to me warning there would be negative press to deal with. And they were very honest that they would edit the way they chose. I was told I could be on screen 24 hours a day or I might not be on at all.

"If you have any skeletons they will come out," they warned.

"Friends and family will be hurt. People will lie about you."

They then told me how to cope, guiding me through everything. I was shitting myself. I kept thinking 'what am I doing here'?

"Once you hit that screen your life will never be the same again," they warned.

Seven to eight million people watched that show. They would know who I was and all my ins and outs.

And I would have no time on my own. Yet I am not a 'people person' because I have no confidence.

I was doing this purely for the money.

You are allowed half a glass of wine or a small beer before going into the Big Brother house.

I had taken loads of pills in the morning so I was already spaced. But there was this runner, a boy who was only about 18. He came in with a bottle of wine to give me a drink – but he popped out and left the bottle, so of course, me being me, I downed it all before he got back. I was steaming, off me rocker!

Then I was put into a car, blindfolded and had earphones put on. I said I didn't want them on because they would mess my hair up, so I was told to just pretend they were on properly.

So there we were driving about 50 yards up the road in a blacked out Mercedes.

I could hear booing – and it was the loudest thing I have ever heard.

"They hate that person, that poor bastard," I said.

And I managed to look up – and saw my face on a huge plasma screen.

They were booing me.

Why? What the fuck had I done wrong?

I knew people sometimes got booed coming out – but not going in!

I was crying in the car saying: "I can't do this."

But Eve, my chaperone, told me to just get out and I would be fine.

I later found out they were booing because of the way my walking video tape (VT) had been edited. It came out as if I had make some joke about fat and ugly people.

But I'm sure what I said, without it being edited, was: "If you are ugly like me, or if you are fat, don't sit and moan about it. Don't keep eating cream cakes. I just stopped eating shit and lost weight."

But it had been edited – and I was hated when I went in.

I was nominated to be kicked out of the house in the second week (but stayed in). Endemol are very clever. They could edit me how they wanted. I was pissed off at the time about how my comments were edited, but I knew that was the chance I took.

I was a mess in that house.

I could not stop crying, even about the most stupid of things; everything was the end of the world. I was depressed, I missed H so much and my BDD was awful. There were mirrors everywhere in there and the lights were so harsh so I was seeing myself constantly. I had never been mirror orientated but now I could see myself 24 hours a day which was absolutely terrible for me. I would try to pull myself together, but to make matters worse there were beautiful women in there: Imogen, Nikki, Jennie, Jayne and Bonnie – young, stunning women with amazing bodies to die for. Suzie was 42 but looked like a 19-year-old. She was older than me but more beautiful than I could ever be.

My other female housemates were Grace, Lisa and Aisleyne.

Then there was me: this crabby, fat old bag who had had loads of surgery. I thought I was a fat, disgusting mess and that made me paranoid beyond belief.

We started with about 20 housemates and I could not have wished to be with better people.

But I was actually going through complete cold turkey from coke and pain killers on air.

And I missed H so much. I worried 'is he being bullied'?

'Have I ruined his life'?

I had no idea what was happening in the outside world.

I kept going to the 'diary room' constantly crying and saying I needed to be with H. The diary room was also a way of escaping everyone else, to get some respite. And if you are depressed it gets you away from the others so you don't depress them.

Big Brother contestants are allowed to nominate three reasons why they should be released from the house. Mine were if H said 'I want my mum home', if H was ill, or if mum was ill.

But H never said those words.

I swear while I was in the Big Brother house it was all showmanship from me. I wasn't Lisa, I wasn't Lea. I don't know who the fuck I was. Sometimes the real me would kick in, then I would lose it again and think to myself 'you are wasting a perfect chance'.

There was a guy in the house called Pete who suffered from Tourette's Syndrome (uncontrollable ticks and outbursts). He was only 24 and had been severely bullied all his life. He was a sweet lad and he reminded me of H, so vulnerable. (But there was also something about his mannerisms that reminded me of Mr Blond). I could relate to him and felt sorry for him – but the media made a big thing about me falling in love with him and made me out to be some sort of bunny boiler. I was not in love with him though I loved him dearly as a friend. Our conversations were edited to make it look as if we had something going. I was not in love with him. What a load of old shit! But he did give me movements in me pantie area! But then again even Dicky did in there because I was incarcerated for nearly three months. Anyone would be gagging for it! I was not in love at all – it was me 'down belows' talking and not me head and me heart.

Pete was completely different from the others. He had a very dark sense of humour, like me, so we got on like a house on fire. As soon as Pete walked into the house I knew instantly 'this boy is going to win'. I think the boys in the house knew that too – that's why they didn't like him.

Glyn, who was Welsh, was adorable, like a baby brother, so vulnerable, but so patriotic, grounded and sorted with his head screwed on. You could phone Glyn any time, 24 hours a day, and he would still be happy and have kind words. When you meet Glyn you get the biggest hug and kiss. He is only 20 years old yet so grown up and mature, one in a million. He really deserves to do well.

Shahbaz should never have been put into the house. He was a very broken person, a very vulnerable, broken soul. I believe for him the Big Brother experience was harmful. I liked him and I tried hard with him – but he was a pain in the arse. The programme was edited to make it look as if we were bullying him, but we weren't. What the viewer didn't see was the way he made a living hell for everybody. It was quite frightening because he could be really nice – then be really nasty and hateful. He would throw things which made you feel threatened and he was horrible to younger members of the house. Considering he was a broken person he was really quite intimidating.

(Anyway he got chucked out by Big Brother in the end, not the public).

Bonnie, from Loughborough, was lovely, a real sweetheart.

There were some people I didn't particularly like, but I didn't hate them.

At one point when I was really down and depressed Aisleyne made some comment about me manipulating the house and using Glyn, so we had a massive bust up. I had to control my temper. If she had said that to me in normal life I would have dropped her. So I thought 'I either walk away or I put you out. I have been spoken to all my life like shit and I am not going to be spoken to like that on national TV and in front of H'.

But I had to walk away, which made me look like a weak person.

If I had reacted it was either stick up for myself and be a bully and knock her out (which I would have) on national telly or walk away and make myself look stupid. So I chose the latter and made myself look ridiculous. Yet if anyone ever says anything about my friends of family I would give my life to protect them.

Being on Big Brother is to be in a confined little bubble, you are not in normal society any more. Even in the first days the producers mess with your head. They change the clocks around so you never know what time it is. This causes sleep deprivation, but if you try and sleep in the day they won't let you. And the temperature is changed so that one minute you're red hot then freezing cold.

The boredom is so bad because everything is so mundane. You are given tasks to do once a week, but they don't last long. One of the tasks that I will always remember was to stand on a big milk crate and not move – while keeping my hands on a plug so the milk wouldn't run out!

We had about half an hour's blindfold dancing to an MP3, which was really funny.

But mostly you find yourself sitting talking to people you do not know (and may not even like). And some people's hygiene was not good, I can tell you.

Sometimes Big Brother took the piss – like locking us out of the house for about six hours in the freezing cold. Or you can be locked in your bedroom for four to five hours.

They keep setting sirens off so you can't sleep. They can wake you up at any time, which really pisses you off, but makes for some funny footage.

And the food was awful. We were living on stuff like Tesco's own brand – on rations. It was basic stuff like rice and pasta. They practically starve you, then give you rations costing about a pound to live on, so your immune system and everything is down, so you would be low and deflated. You would then win a task, then they give you sugary shit and more 'e' numbers than you know what to do with – so you would be wizzing off your tits. Food becomes a huge thing in the house, but you're not able to exercise. Before I went on Big Brother I was not a big eater and had actually lost two stones while I was in Belgium.

I know I am not the most beautiful (more of an oil slick than an oil painting). I know I am damn ugly. But when I went into the

Big Brother house I wasn't fat so I knew at least no one could slag me off about my weight. I can cope with the ugly thing, but not the fat thing. I thought 'they can slag me off about my face, my boobs – but not about being fat'. I weighed just over eight stones when I went in.

But sitting on my arse eating biscuits, crisps, bread and jam resulted in me putting on three and a half stones in the house. If I eat normally I put on weight easily, so when I came out I was three to four stones heavier. And I had got used to eating so that made it harder for me to lose weight after Big Brother.

My lowest point came in about week three or four. I dreamt that H was going to school and I woke up thinking he was late. I had never been away from him for ten years, but when I woke up he wasn't there and that really freaked me out.

When I went into the BB house I think I was the fifth one in and I thought: "Oh my fucking God, what have I just done with my life?"

Then some more new housemates came in.

The door at the bottom of the stairs opened – and there he stood. My dream bloke: tall, tanned, built like a brick shithouse, bald and swinging handcuffs round like a bitch.

I think it took me a few seconds before I realised 'Oh shit, he's gay'.

Why are all the best looking guys in this world gay?

And there he stood – Richard Newman – my Dicky.

I looked at him and he looked at me and that was it.

When Rich first walked in the house he shouted at the top of his voice: "You look like Dolly Parton!"

So of course it stuck.

What a compliment for me – and an insult for poor old Dolly Parton though!

And me and Rich have been inseparable since.

In the house you are locked up in rooms for hours so all you have to do is talk to housemates and the bitchiness is unbelievable.

Once Grace and Imogen or Nicki were in the bedroom and I could hear them saying things like: "She makes me feel physically sick", "she is horrible". Then Grace came out of the bedroom and wanted me to give her a hug, which I did. I can remember telling Rich about it, but he told me I was just being paranoid. But I know what I heard and I know it was about me.

Me and Rich had some good times in the house, but we went through a bad patch because I believed what other people were saying: that he was slagging me off and not to trust him. I was horrible to Rich in the house because I believed he was being horrible about me.

At times like that I would cry in bed thinking 'What the fuck are you doing in the house? You're a freak anyway?'

The arguments between us were well publicised. Now I know better. I will always take the word of my friends.

I was constantly in the diary room saying 'I'm going and you can't stop me!'

Me and Rich were nominated for eviction from Big Brother together, so it was called the Clash of the Titans in the press. Whichever one of us was voted out would mean I would not see my soul mate for a while. I was the one to go and I could not even look at Rich without crying because he meant so much to me.

On the night before the eviction *Big Brother* gave us a 'Dicky and Dolly' dinner party in the house – the last supper. I gave a speech and said how much I loved everyone.

I was evicted from the house after eight weeks.

I had been made to come to terms with the person I was and it had made me stronger.

While I was in the house it was a surreal environment with people telling you what to do and you lose control of your own life. I had been in controlling relationships, but I knew the Big Brother situation would not last for ever.

By then I had got used to the surroundings, and even though I missed H, by the end of eight weeks I actually didn't want to leave the house. I thought they were my friends in there and I was quite frightened to get back to normal life.

I didn't know what had happened out there. We had no access to newspapers, radio, phones or TV, so one of the scariest things was walking up those steps up to the doors leading to the outside world.

I can remember all my housemates sang *I Will Survive* by Gloria Gaynor as I walked up the stairs, because they know that was my favourite song.

I could hear a few boos, but I could also hear some cheers. I was aware there were crowds outside so it was just the scariest thing – so scary it stops you breathing. I swear my heart stopped beating for a few seconds in fright. I felt physically sick and the adrenalin was really pumping.

And I waited for what seemed like ages for the doors to open – unaware that people could still hear me at that point. I knew I had the mic attached, but I thought they would switch it on when I got to the studio interview. But no, even that part of my eviction waiting for the doors to open was being relayed on live TV. It was only a few seconds but it seemed like ages.

So most people remember those immortal words just before I got out: "For God's sake open the doors you cunts!"

I would never have said that if I had known it was being broadcast live before the watershed. So people were phoning Ofcom to complain.

I was booed when I went in – but cheered when I came out!

It was the most surreal experience stepping out in front of those crowds. There were about 300–400 people; there were flashing lights and banners. I looked down the stairs desperate to see my friends and family. I had been away from H for 11 weeks – taken out of circulation from society and put in the company of just 12 people.

Then, in complete contrast I was standing in front of hundreds of people, including the paparazzi with their cameras flashing.

I was a normal, everyday person when I went in; now seven million people knew who I was. It was daunting, but at the same time the best feeling you could ever imagine. Even though there was some bad publicity in the tabloids the general public have been fantastic to me. People on websites slag you off, but once they know you as a person face to face it's different.

The presenter Davina McCall was at the bottom of the stairs. She grabbed me – and put her head straight in my boobs!

I was then interviewed by Davina; and looking back I feel the interview was crap – because I was so frightened. My nerves were shattered, I was paranoid beyond belief and suffering from a nervous breakdown at the time.

I was so shocked by the whirlwind that followed. It was unbelievable. It seems when you leave Big Brother you are either vilified or put on a pedestal. While I was in the house my character was vilified from day one because of the adult movie. Endemol wanted me out in the first week, but the housemates did not nominate me.

The psychologist Steven (who is lovely) talked to me and showed me a load of press clippings.

I looked at the pile of clippings and said: "Oh my God. Are they all our cuttings (thinking they were about all of us)?"

"No. These are all yours!" came the reply.

When I read them they were all focussing on the porn film – saying what a bad mum I was and that I was an alcoholic. I had been ripped to bits in the press and I was devastated.

Hand on heart – I never thought in a million years that film would come out. I reasoned 'why would anyone make a shit film and keep the footage?'

I'm not proud of what I did – but when I read those cuttings I felt sick. In fairness to Endemol all I can say is Big Brother contestants know what they are letting themselves in for. They warn you there is a chance you will get bad press.

"Are you alright?" Steven asked.

"All I care about is H and me mum, and whether H has been bullied," I said.

I didn't give a shit about what anyone said about me. I have been ripped to bits by the best of 'em, but I only get affected by words when they are from people I think love me. So I coped with the cuttings.

Then I rang H.

I remember him crying and sobbing, saying he missed me.

Then I spoke to mum and she cried too.

When I was evicted it was between me and Rich. H revealed he had been one of those who voted to keep Rich in – so he could get me back home!

Security guards were ushering around me and I was taken away in a car with the windows blacked out. (I can see how all this would go to some people's heads and it has for some). I decided to enjoy it while it lasted. This showbiz razzmatazz was not going to last forever; there would come a time when I would have to work. After all, I only went on Big Brother for the money in the first place.

I was taken to a beautiful hotel in the countryside, Sopwell House where I was treated like royalty. When I arrived my so-called 'friends' were there. But the people I really wanted to see: my mum, H and my best friend Jade were not there. Jade was absolutely devastated at not being invited. I truly believe my 'friends' wanted to ruin my eviction night. They knew exactly what they were doing, having already sold their stories about me, making money off me, taking the piss out of me so they could be on telly.

There were about five of my so-called friends there.

There was one girl in particular I was not pleased to see and I could not understand why she was there at all.

Mr Blond was there so I asked him: "What the hell is she doing here?"

I suspected she was invited just to ruin my night.

It should have been a celebration night – but I cried because I wanted to be back in the house. I would rather be back there than have these people I didn't like around me.

I had left Rich, Pete, Nikki and Aisleyne at the time I thought – these were my best friends. I just sat there in a chair crying watching Big Brother – watching my friends. It was heartbreaking, awful.

I looked around the beautiful room in the hotel. It was now empty, strewn with empty bottles of wine and bits of food. This was my night, my eviction and there was just one glass of pink champagne left for me. They had eaten all of the food and drank all the wine. They had taken the piss and I didn't want them near me. Mr Blond confirmed they had sold stories on me and he told me how much they had made and how they had taken the piss out of me. So I asked him to tell them to go.

It should have been the most exciting night of my life, but it was completely and utterly ruined by my so-called mates. Everyone it seems shits on me, no matter what I try to do.

To make matters worse me and Mr Blond had a massive argument that night because he had allowed 'her' to be at the party. I felt I didn't like anybody and all I wanted to do was go back to mum and H.

The following morning I had to do an exclusive photo shoot for a tabloid newspaper and I really did not want to do it.

I got up in the morning, weighed myself and looked at myself in the mirror – then sat on the bathroom floor next to the scales and bawled my eyes out.

Mr Blond was downstairs at the time.

I phoned H but could hardly speak because I was crying, so I told him I had got a cold and was really tired.

On the way downstairs to the photo shoot I had a call from Endemol telling me to be careful with the tab – because my 'friends' had spent over £2,000 on it. They had ordered the best champagne and wine and all the food they could. I felt two inches tall and was really apologetic.

I hated the photo shoot because I was so fat and because what should have been a really happy time for me was so sad.

Me and Mr Blond stayed at Sopwell House that night. He was convinced me and Pete were going to get together, but he was more like a brother to me.

Perhaps there were times on Big Brother when my feelings for him got a bit too much, but I managed to pull them back.

Call me shallow, but my guys have to be over 6ft, built like a brick shit house and have tattoos – that is what I find physically attractive.

The next day I was moved to the Holiday Inn at Elstree and that's where I saw mum and H for the first time.

As soon as the door opened I was so excited. H was streaming with tears. He was only ten and he had drawn me a card, and bought me a teddy and flowers. Mum was crying too. The first thing H said when he stopped crying was: "I am proud of you mum."

That meant more to me than anything you could ever imagine.

I said: "Are you alright? Have you been bullied?

He said: "No. I'm famous at school!"

I asked them: "Are you alright with everything?"

Mum said: "We are behind you 100 per cent. I'm proud of you."

Mum gave me a hug – and then I felt at ease.

And I thought: 'I am going to have a damn good go at this and make it work'.

A whirlwind of TV, papers, magazines and radio followed.

I am quite opinionated and I knew I could present and broadcast. So I decided there and then to settle down, to buckle down and make a good life for H and me mum.

I came out of the house clean – but went straight back into my ways.

But I have also worked hard ever since.

During week 11 of Big Brother after I had been out of the house for three weeks I was at a double glazing factory buying some windows and a conservatory when my phone rang. It was Endemol asking if I would consider going back into 'the house'!

They were going to try something new: holding a public vote to see who they would like to see again.

I knew now that H and mum were alright and as I had loads of work booked up I thought this would boost my profile. I would also earn more money so I had nothing to lose.

I said 'yes' so they said: "We need you back at Elstree."

A train was booked for me and a car picked me up. Instead of going into the actual 'house' we were housed in a little apartment at the side of it.

We all had to record a 30-minute plea saying why we should go back in. The publicity to get us back in lasted for about three days.

All the housemates who had been evicted so far had to line up. It was the most nerve-racking thing. It took place on air. We were able to meet up with the housemates again on the Big Brother double eviction night when Suzi and Mikey were evicted.

Nikki, who was in love with Pete, knew how to play the game by then. She knew how to manipulate people and how to get Rich round her little finger. She sat on his knee and whispered to him: "If I don't get into the house give 'Petee' my heart and tell him I love him."

So I went into the diary room and said: "We might all as well go now, she's done it."

First Sam was called up – and told no, she was not going back in.

Then it was Grace's turn. Yes, she was in.

Then it was my turn. Davina knew I was petrified. She came up to me and said: "Oh Lea, I'm so sorry – but you're in!"

Me, Nikki, Grace and Mikey were all voted back in.

Rich, who always thought of others, took Nikki in because Pete was really down at the time and he wanted to make sure he was alright.

I was so excited knowing I was going to see Rich again. I missed this man more than anything. The only people I missed more were H and me mum.

Anyway I was back in the house for a further four days. It was still quite stressful, but this time I thought 'enjoy it now'. The press could not slay me anymore; and the public had accepted me. I had been out of the house for three weeks and had more confidence. I knew I could overcome my problems and I think that is when I started to learn to deal with my dysmorphia.

And I was back with Rich – someone who has an aura about him. Rich hasn't got a bad bone in his body. He is brutally honest but never judges me. He says if he is offending me it is only because he is trying to help. And he has promised he will always be honest with me. Since I mct Rich my life has been 1,000 per cent better; I have had such a laugh with him, pissing about and getting drunk.

And looking back I had some amazing times with some amazing people. Me, Rich and Glyn were particularly close. I know I am so fortunate because there were so many others who wanted to be in my place.

Pete won Big Brother – and £100,000. Glyn came second.

The show was one of the most popular Big Brother series ever, the final week being watched by millions.

Me and Rich came out of Big Brother best friends. We are inseparable and even if we lose touch in years to come I know we will get back together. At the time of writing it is nearly three years since Big Brother and there is not one day when we haven't seen or phoned each other.

I have never looked back. Big Brother, by giving me that chance, has turned everything round tenfold. Looking back, I am now a completely and utterly different person and it frightens me to think that I was such a mess. Without a doubt I would not have had the life I have without Big Brother. In fact I would probably be dead. Before I went into the house I had had enough; I could not see any way out of anything.

I have watched bits of the Big Brother footage, but not watched it properly. I've watched about half an hour of snippets just to see the other housemates.

# Finding Love (That Old Chestnut)

I guess it's hard for most people to find love, especially nowadays. But it's even harder for a sufferer of BDD to find somebody – and actually keep them.

You're constantly paranoid that you're fat, you're ugly, you're worthless – so to actually meet and have a relationship with someone is difficult on both sides because the other partner is constantly being bombarded with all your insecurities and hatred. If any of my ex's looked at other girls and made comments I was fine with the looking, but not the comments. They would say things like 'Christ look at her', 'my God, look at her tits, they're huge', 'wish you looked like that, she's got gorgeous tits' or 'she's got gorgeous legs'.

Don't forget all this was spoken directly to me, so of course I was going to be bloody upset and insecure, so we would argue all the time.

Holidays were the worse as I had to be in my bikini or something during the day. I used to love going on holiday but also hate it because it was a nightmare for me.

To sit around the pool or on the beach and see all these stunning, gorgeous, toned, big-boobed women – and then you had me – this short, fat lump hiding under me towel all day and sweating like a pig because I was too scared to go in the sea or pool in case anyone saw me. I know nobody gave a shit – but I did. My mind was made up. I would sit there all day and not move.

To see women going topless was a million times worse because I had bigger heat bumps on me back than I had boobies on me chest. And I'd cop me fellas always having a crafty look.

One of them was so bad. I remember him lying on his belly on the sunbed with his sunglasses on, pretending to be asleep. But the knob didn't know I could see his eyes. What an asshole.

And I knew who he was ogling at. There was a group of girls opposite the pool topless – beautiful all of them with bodies to die for. He would even pretend to snore for crying out loud!

This geezer was such a dumpty. So I lay there watching him, not saying a word because I didn't want to be shouted at or put down. So I just tortured myself mentally instead.

Then it happened. One of the hotel rep's came up behind him and threw ice cold water on him. He jumped up in shock.

Are you ready for this?

He jumped up with a bloody hard on poking out the top of his trunks.

Class or what?

And of course the rep' saw it and made such a massive deal about it everyone was staring at us. I felt so ashamed and humiliated. We argued for the rest of the holiday after that.

All I want is the same as everyone else: just to be loved and wanted, to be treated like a princess and not hurt. I know I go for wrong 'uns in the bloke department but I can't seem to help it. Guess I'm just a bloody shit magnet. My friends say I just need to find a normal nine to five guy – but I've tried and nothing seems to happen.

I don't think I ever will find a man, to be honest, because I come with far too much baggage. Firstly they have to love me for me, warts and all. Then H has to like them, then my mum has to like them. Then they have to accept my friends and the way I look. Hmmm. Now can you see why I'm still single at 38 years cowing old?

If you suffer from BDD try and sit down and explain what you are going through with your partner instead of completely shutting them out and dismissing them.

Because they can help you and make you learn to like yourself, even if only a little bit.

Also, if you are with a sufferer and didn't know – but now you see some of the signs, perhaps now you can take notice and deal with the situation.

Just sit down and talk, because talking is the best cure.

Don't be judgemental and don't keep saying 'but you're mad, there's nothing wrong with you'. And never say 'but you know you're not fat and ugly'. Because even though you think you're being nice and kind we take that very badly. It's as if you don't believe how we really feel. So just let your partner speak, without interjection, until the time is right. Then just hold that person tight, even if you have fallen out. It's not our fault and it's not yours either. Just try to understand.

My fairytale will never come true. My chance of meeting my soul mate has gone; so have the dreams of a beautiful wedding with my man standing there loving me.

But don't let yours go. Fight for it tooth and nail – and hold on in there – because love is the greatest cure for anything.

Never in a million years do I think I will ever find my Prince Charming, my Mr Right, my soul mate. It used to really play on my mind and get me down before, especially when I watched films or even TV shows – watching what I had always dreamed of and my heart longed for, wanting it so bad it hurt. But now it doesn't seem to hurt so much. Perhaps I'm now at an age when I'm used to being alone: me and my thoughts and dreams in bed at night instead of having Mr Right holding me.

You know when you're little and all you want is a beautiful wedding so you can be a princess and your man will love you forever and ever?

Well, you soon grow out of that little scenario. I did anyway – especially the bit about the man loving you 'for ever and ever'.

I think with all my ex-partners I was so desperate to be loved and wanted that I put up with all their shite, waiting for the day when the punches would stop, the mental abuse would be a thing of the past and they would love me.

But I was a twat. That day never came from any of them.

God I was so desperate to be loved.

What an arse I was.

I ruined 20 years of my life on those vile losers and I will never get those years back.

But one good thing to come out of my car crash relationships (if you can call it 'good') is I will NEVER be a punch bag and doormat again.

# Life After Big Brother

When you come out of Big Brother you are assigned an agent. They try and pick one which they think will be suited to you. Mine was a very ruthless lady working in the industry in London.

She made a lot of money out of Big Brother contestants and good on her – but our relationship only lasted for about four months and I now represent myself.

I was new to this and didn't have a clue about what was going to happen. When you come out you don't even realise you're famous because you go into the house as one person and think that you come out the same. But when eight million people know who you are and everything about you – and you are never going to be that same person again.

My first taste of this was when I made my way back to Nottingham by car and stopped at a service station with Mr Blond. I came out of the house on a Friday and this was a Tuesday, four days later. I got out of the car and was bombarded with people. I was absolutely petrified. I ended up with hundreds of people round me wanting autographs and to be photographed with me. This was my first glimpse of what was to come.

I just thought: "Oh my God! What the hell…"

Mr Blond managed to get me back into the car and he said: "Oh my God. That was the most surreal thing I have ever seen in my life."

It was actually hard to put it into words. Everyone was being nice, but it's amazing to think they know who you are.

And ever since, the British public have always been nice to me. I have never had one person say anything bad to me. I often question myself why they are being nice and why they like me.

People say to me 'if you weren't a nice person they would dislike you'.

And all I ever really want is to help people. I never ask for anything from anybody. All I want is to be happy.

The day after I came out of the house I had to attend Carphone Warehouse in Nottingham to have pictures taken and sign photos.

I thought to myself 'no one will turn up'.

But when I arrived I was driven round the back of the building and there were police there with the roads all cordoned off. Every road was packed with people – and they had all come to see me! I had never seen so many in my life and I was shitting myself. I was supposed to be there for an hour. I was there for about five hours and there were still people being turned away; it was just surreal.

And that night I had to do a personal appearance at a nightclub. It was really weird to see all these people who had turned up to see me. They were shouting 'get your tits out' but nothing nasty. It was actually lovely to be around nice people.

And since that day I have never been around nasty people. Since Big Brother the nasty people seem to have dwindled away, just vanished. It's as if Big Brother was like a fairy godmother who banished all the bad people away, leaving me only with the good ones.

Then I had to do magazine deals and photo shoots. Companies pay me to have my hair done (I have had hair extensions). I get free clothes and shoes courtesy of different companies.

And I get to meet famous people who are on the telly. Just because they are on TV people seem to forget they are normal people. I met Allan Carr and Justin Lee Collins from the Friday Night Project. I was such a fan of theirs and got to meet them when I was invited on the show. We all went out together that night and I got on like a house on fire with them. Me, Alan and Justin have been good friends ever since. Alan has even been on *The Dickie and Dolly Show*. They are all nice guys, the nicest you will ever meet in show business with no air of arrogance. They don't think they are better than anyone else; they are just normal, lovely guys with hearts of gold. They could put on airs and be horrible – but they don't. They are doing so well and deserve all the happiness. When good things happen to good people you know God is doing his job properly.

Two and a half years after Big Brother this is all still going on. I have not stopped working.

The highlight has to be hosting London Gay Pride this year. To stand on stage and look out at Trafalgar Square seeing all those people, and to be accepted into gay society, is one of the most amazing things. Gay people have made me feel I deserve to be alive. I am different and do live my life differently to the norm, and I am accepted by them. I have attended Gay Pride in Belfast, Birmingham – many places up and down the country – and the reaction from the crowd is always absolutely brilliant.

And it turns out so many gay people, male and female, have dysmorphia. With men I suppose it's because a lot of them think gay men want muscle boys – so their body image is at an all-time low. A lot of them think they do not look good enough for a gay guy to love them or want to be with them.

All the gay guys I have met have been beautiful, but have no self worth. It's awful to listen to them. My dysmorphia does not matter to me, but to listen to others going through their pain and not being able to stop it is horrible. I can't put anything into their head – just like people can't put it into mine.

I got a job presenting a weekly show on London based Gaydar Radio and loved that; it is one of the best jobs I have ever done. I worked as a broadcaster with Rich and our 'Dicky and Dolly' show ran for two years. We would chat and have special guests – interviewing some of the great '80s icons. I even got to meet and interview Samantha Fox – the woman I idolised all my adult life. And she is still stunning. I also got involved with Stonewalls, a great charity which raises awareness about gay equality.

I have attended beauty pageants and people offer me work via MySpace. Going to jobs seems to create more opportunities and I have work coming up abroad. I am just so lucky.

I have met Cleo Roccos, (who was Kenny Everett's best friend in the world) who I admired and the actor Sir Ian McKellen – and many more, too many to mention.

And I have enjoyed doing everything: whether it's opening a bed shop or standing on a stage in front of 85,000 people. I really could not wish for any more.

I came out of Big Brother in 2006 and only one thing has marred my happiness.

In November 2007 I was shopping with my mum in Tesco in Nottingham when one of my mum's old friends came up to us. We hadn't seen her for years.

"I'm sorry about Ginny dying," the woman said.

Ginny, my Mammar.

"No, you've got that wrong," mum said. "Of course she's not dead; we'd have been told."

This really upset mum. This was her mum after all.

We asked the lady how she knew Mammar had died and she said she had gone to the cemetery to visit someone when she saw Mammar's name had been added to the other side of the book on grandad's grave.

Me and mum went home, still convinced that the lady had got it wrong. But when we got home mum phoned Cliff – who confirmed Mammar had passed away.

She had died in 2001.

We had been to grandad's grave, but there had been a couple of years when things were so hectic with the way my life had been that we had not visited.

Mammar's name had not been added until 2007. We both just cried.

We went to the visit the grave, but since our last visit a couple of years ago the area had changed. Shrubs had been put in and trees planted and it all looked so different that we had trouble finding the grave and I was getting hysterical.

But eventually we found it – and there it was. Ginny's name had been added. It was absolutely horrible and I knew that my mum was breaking inside.

Mammar's wish was never to die without her make-up on. Her worse fear was to die with no make-up on, not 'done up' – as she thought when she died grandad would be waiting at the pearly gates. And my grandad had never seen her without make-up on. We have since found out she died in a hospice on her own. She would not have had her hair done, her nails varnished or her make-up on – and we never got to tell her that we loved her.

I would like to think we could have resolved the situation, but my family is cold-hearted and emotionless. I would so love to be in a 'normal' family. When you see others being happy it's not nice to be in such a hard, cold family.

The day Lynn took Mammar was heart wrenching for me and mum because we loved her and doted on her. Men were not a big part of our lives then – Mammar had lost grandad and mum had lost Cliff, so me, Mammar and mum brought up H.

Grandad and Mammar used to love heather so I take some to the grave now and plant bulbs there. But finding out that way about Mammar still hurts mum to this day.

# Me and My BDD

I won't let my BDD control me anymore – because now I can control it.

I hear so-called experts in this and that saying 'oh she still has surgery. She's still changing her appearance'.

Durr, no shit Sherlock. Of course I am. It's because I CHOOSE to, because I like to: nothing else, no other reason – unlike before when my BDD started when I was little, like I said earlier in the book.

It did control me: for all my childhood years, as a teenager, and through my 20s until about two years ago to be totally honest with you. I know my BDD made it difficult in my relationships, especially in the bedroom department which caused so many arguments in every relationship I had.

Just the thought of having to be naked horrified me: to think my partner (whichever one it was) would have to see my flabby fat ass and saggy body made my heart race. I would work myself up so much and get in a complete state over trying to think up an excuse to have an argument. Then I wouldn't have to have sex or be naked.

The amount of times I would say 'oh, I'm on my period' or 'I have a toothache'. But the best one was 'I promise tomorrow I will make it really special for you'.

Of course tomorrow never came around, thank God.

I can remember the feeling of relief when I knew I'd got away with it again. I'd get so excited it felt like Christmas, just knowing 'yep, I've done it. I don't have to get undressed and do the deed!'

The feeling of panic, the hot flushes and feeling sick to my stomach had all gone and turned into euphoria. God I was good! And I would lie in bed giggling in my head like a little girl.

Mornings used to be such hard work for me as I could never, not in a billion years, ever let any of my ex-partners see me with no make-up on or without my hair being perfect.

I would set my alarm at least two, maybe three hours earlier than I should have, just to cake my face up in so much crap. I would get through more foundation and powder in a week than ten women would in a month.

Foundation, powder, more foundation, more powder, time after time. My poor skin: all my pores completely blocked and starved of oxygen.

Then I'd start with my black eyeliner. Oh dear God. Alice Cooper or Gene Simmons from the group Kiss had nothing on me. I was walking round with permanent black eyes, as if I'd been in a boxing ring with Mike Tyson. I'd put on so much mascara that sometimes all my lashes would become one huge clump. Then I would have to take off all my make-up again.

The amount of arguments I would have with myself! I would scream at myself out loud: "You stupid bitch. Now look what you've done. What did you do that for? Why did you do that?"

I was a different person when my dysmorphia took over. I was like the devil. I would scream and shout at myself and anyone close to me. I was vile and I know that now. But at the time all I cared about was hating myself and that self hatred would completely take me over and no one could stand in my way. If a tiny piece of hair did not look right I would completely ruin it with my hands or brush, then drench it with even more hairspray.

Then I'd just sit and pull it until big clumps came out.

It didn't matter what day of the week it was or what time, getting ready for school or work was hell because I knew I had to go out in public. So I would wind myself up the night before, knowing I had to get up and go through the same old shit day after day. It was torture.

Some days I would sit in the bath and scrub my skin with the nail brush until it bled. Other times I wouldn't even take my clothes off in the bath because I couldn't bear to be naked.

I would say to myself: 'Just get in the bath in your nightie then you don't have to look at your nasty fat legs wobbling in the water'.

Coping with dysmorphia as a child, especially in the '70s and '80s was a living hell. Nowadays kids are completely clued up on issues to do with just about anything. You could ask a child as young as six or seven what anorexia or bulimia is and I bet nine out of ten would know.

But 30 years ago there was nothing in the media. Nobody ever spoke about body image and eating disorders – apart from the singer Karen Carpenter who died from anorexia in the '70s.

Only the other day I sat with me mam talking about my childhood and how I used to feel inside, how alone I was, trapped in my head hating this face and body. She didn't have a clue.

She was a fantastic mum, just quite distant. I know now she loved me, but at the time I didn't. I needed my mum and dad to be loving. I wish I hadn't been too scared to ask them why I felt so angry inside, why I didn't like my reflection and why I couldn't stop hurting myself. I should have been able to ask mum 'what's wrong with me?', 'Does everyone feel like this?', 'Is this what life is?'

How the hell did I know? I was only seven for crying out loud. Even at that young age I felt I wasn't normal and was completely consumed with self loathing, so much that the anger inside hurt my head. I was so enraged that sometimes I would just flip for no reason whatsoever. The things I would say and do to anyone around me…

And even today, though I control my BDD, once in a while IT will sneak out – even if only for a millisecond. It's as though IT still wants me to know 'I'm still here and I'm going nowhere love'. Then I get, like a second wave, and IT has gone again as quickly as IT came.

But it wasn't always like this.

Years ago I was like the devil, a bloody mad banshee screaming at myself or at whoever was in the house with me at the time.

Sometimes things would start off as a nice, normal day. Then IT would rear ITS head and the 'voice' (I say 'voice' loosely because I knew it was my thoughts in my head, not anyone else's voice) would say the most evil things to me as if wanting to destroy me. And I don't have a clue why.

It was as if my brain was telling me: "Don't go out, you're too ugly, you're too fat. Why don't you just kill yourself? Go on, you know you want to. Stop being a chicken and do it. No one will miss you. Nobody cares if you die."

Then I'd cry uncontrollably for hours in complete turmoil with my head banging so much my eyes hurt.

Sometimes these bad times could go on for days. Other times I would just get on with it as if my head and body were saying 'Just deal with it. Don't think about it. Just STOP it'.

I did sometimes – but not as much as I would have liked.

My temper would flare if I couldn't get into a pair of jeans or if my hair or face weren't right. On the worse days I would physically punch myself in the face or hit myself with objects on my body, head and face – with anything at close range – a can of hairspray, brushes, mirrors, shoes, anything that I knew would mark my skin.

Even at junior school I realised there was something not quite right with me.

It's difficult to explain why I acted the way I did. People who don't suffer with BDD don't understand it's not something you can just turn off.

And it's not me saying 'oh please feel sorry for me'. We don't want – and we hate – compliments. Sufferers are not attention seekers. It makes me so fucking angry when people say 'you're after sympathy' or 'stop attention seeking'.

If you don't ask me questions then I don't need to bleeding answer them do I?

And don't expect me to lie. I will always be honest, truthful and above board.

So NO. It's not an 'oh please feel sorry for me' illness. It's just called the truth, so deal with it.

# True friends

I remember someone saying to me years ago: "When you're older you'll be able to count your true friends on two hands, maybe even one."

How true that turned out to be.

I don't have a big family and the one I have is not close at all. So my friends are my family to me. Growing up you think your best friends will always be there. For some people I guess they are. But for me, like most people in this world, you lose them.

When I was in my teens my so called best mate turned into a bitch. That's all I'm saying about that vile slag. That should have shown me what some people are really like. But oh no, not me. I had to keep trusting and trusting didn't I?

I met a friend through an acquaintance and she seemed really lovely. I trusted her. And trust for me is such a huge big deal. I knew her for about three years and loved her dearly. She did freak me out on a number of occasions though. I remember having my hair done differently – and a couple of days later hers was the same. That should have made me go 'Woah, woah, woaho. What's happening here?' But nope, I didn't.

Then she would buy exactly the same clothes, boots, shoes, bags – everything. She would ring me and say: "So what are you wearing today?"

Then she would turn up in the same sodding stuff.

If that wasn't bad enough she bought the same car, even the same colour.

To top it off she decorated her bloody house the same. That did freak me out.

I wish someone at the time would have said: "Sort that mate of yours out will ya."

"And don't you think it's a bit weird that your fella is always round hers and giving her lifts?"

But nobody did.

I couldn't see the wood for the trees could I?

Because all I wanted was for him to love me and be with me. So I didn't mind that they spent time together because she was my best friend and he was my fella. So of course, I didn't think for two seconds what they were really up to.

Then the day came when I found a letter she wrote to him pleading her undying love for him saying 'please just leave her'.

Leave me? Oh my fucking God. My gob was on the floor. Talk about feeling like a prize tit.

When he came home I showed him the letter I had found in his jeans pocket. And the first thing he said was: "What are you going through my stuff for?"

Excuse me – I was doing the washing you knob end, so I checked there wasn't anything in the pockets.

Out came all the lies: "She's a nutter, a stalker. She won't leave me alone. I haven't done anything with her. I hate her, but she just keeps bugging me."

"Fine, OK. I'll ring her," I said.

To cut a very long story short she came round and he admitted it.

So we split up and they got together for a few months. But little did she know – until now that is – that we saw each other a few times (if you know what I mean) in the bedroom department until I told him to piss off. So Little Miss Perfect if you're reading my book: sorry love but he came back to me till I shooed him off.

That's why I find it hard to trust people because of the pain of that little episode.

What happened next shouldn't have been a surprise really.

When I got Big Brother 7 I thought I had such a brilliant circle of friends. There were only about five or six of them, but I really honestly thought we were close.

I think if I was to meet me I'd give myself a right kick up the ass.

You see, I didn't know at the time how this whole Big Brother thing worked. Even though I had watched it I didn't really get into it and never read the mags and 'red tops' (tabloids).

My so-called best friends, apart from Jade, sold me out again – this time for a few measly quid.

Jade has to be my oldest, truest friend in the world. We are more like sisters than mates. Her life has been so much like mine. I think that's why I love her so much. She's a struggling single mum with her little girl Ellie Ray. Like me, she has had the same man trouble to a tee.

She could have made a fortune out of me when I was in 'the house' – with her photos and what we used to get up to. And trust me, she really needed the cash more than anyone I know. But she didn't sell a thing on me.

We're closer now than we have ever been and we have been friends for about ten years. I know she's going nowhere and will never hurt me. She's me rock is our Jadeykins. I can count my true friends on one hand these days.

A true friend is for life no matter what and I have found that in Rich.

We work together all the time under our stage names Dicky and Dolly.

I can't imagine my life without Dicky. He has been me left leg since we met – a true soul mate. He knows me inside out and there's nothing we wouldn't do for each other – well apart from the rumpy pumpy side but I'm still working on that.

Since leaving the BB house we met some amazing, true, honest friends: Jane, Wanda and Jenna are the main ones. I'm so blessed. I have the family I always dreamed of in my friends. I now have the sisters I longed for and my brother to give me the cuddles I missed.

So be wary of some of your friends, but hold tight to others as they will be your friends for life.

# Stop hurting

Abuse has many ugly faces: from insults to full blown beatings. For years I was subjected to mental and physical abuse – from such an early age that I just took it as the norm.

And it's OK for all these do-gooders and experts saying this, that and the other – but unless they have been through, or are going through, abuse how the hell can they know your pain and your fears? I'm sorry, but no amount of reading books will ever put them in the place of someone being abused.

If you listen to some people and talk to them they think that the only abuse is physical. But that is so far from the truth. Mental abuse is just complete torture from the second you wake up to the time you try to sleep again. But then, sleep doesn't come easily.

I think my BDD contributed to my weakness more than I like to admit. But if you're with a partner and they know you, your insecurities, your weak points, they can attack them and make your feeling of worthlessness 1,000 times worse.

Some people think that name calling is only that – but it cuts you to the bone and messes your head up and can turn you into a wreck.

Abuse starts with:

'What's the matter with you? Are you completely thick and stupid? Can't you ever do anything right?'

And it continues:

'Just look at yourself. How can I be seen with you? You're a mess. Can't you lose weight? Fucking hell, you're so ugly you're lucky to have me – 'cause nobody else would have you. You're an ugly mess, useless at everything.'

I could go on until the cows come home with the mind games I've endured.

Struggling with BDD is mentally draining enough; and I think that all anybody wants in this life is just to be loved, so we put up with all the shit that is thrown at us.

I did keep telling myself it would stop and that I just had to hang on in there. I would tell myself it didn't matter how much I hurt because one day he would want me and love me.

But it doesn't work like that.

The mental abuse turns into physical abuse.

I remember the first beating I got from my so-called fella. Shit, I was only young, a teenager. And if I had a daughter, or if H went through what I was subjected to, I couldn't be held responsible for what I'd do to that person. I'm not saying that's right, but no one in this world should have to suffer at the hands of another.

I remember at the time thinking it was all my fault – that I had made him hit me because he was ashamed of me and I embarrassed him because I was fat and ugly.

But as time goes by in relationships you get older and a bit stronger.

I can honestly say that in my relationships I've only been with one fella who didn't hit me for the sake of it. His temper was down to drugs – a lot of them.

But no matter what abuse you might be put through – you shouldn't be.

I can't tell you what to do, only tell you what I had to go through. So maybe you will see an end to your abuse, because trust me, years ago I could never see an end to it. I never thought of myself as a weak person until I was made weak by others. And that's my fault because I allowed it to happen to me. I'm not saying when I was younger I could have stopped it, but when I was in my late 20s and 30s I could have.

And I did find it in me to stop it.

# Today

I t's not rocket science to say you only have one mum – and no matter what you should always love them.

And if you can, look after them as they have and do look after you.

My mum has had such a crap, horrible, lonely life, but she's always tried to make others happy. She was never really there for me when I was younger, and she will openly say that as well, but how could she when she was going through hell in her marriage and felt worthless herself? But as soon as I had H it was as if our lives were inseparable and I can't imagine life without her.

I know she is a right pain in the ass but I would never change her for the world. Mum is with me forever – that's the way it stays. Whatever Cliff did to mum she is happy and settled now.

Cliff is with 'George' now, a lovely girl and really good friend of mine, a sweetheart. They have a little boy Tom, who is 11. He is a right little belter, really lovely. Cliff and George make each other happy.

And after all that sadness I am grateful that George has given Cliff happiness.

I just wish that my mum had found somebody to be happy with too – but she has me, H and the 'boys' (my dogs) God help her. And she has stood by me these last few years and when my BDD has been really bad.

My son H. What can I say? They broke the mould when I made him.

He is a life saver. He has helped me to love. He is the reason I still breathe.

Parents say they love their kids and would do anything for them. I would give my life for my child; he means so much to me.

We have both been to hell and back. He is such an adult, and I feel guilty he has grown up so quickly and for what I put him through (though not on purpose). I didn't want him to see me such a wreck.

H is only 13. He is so funny, so caring and so clever. I know every parent will say that; but he is the most clued up child. He gives me cuddles constantly, tells me he loves me (even in front of his mates) and he looks a little bit like me (poor little fucker).

But he has got his dad's mannerisms, mood swings and temper and is built like a brick shit house, proper sturdy, tall and big boned. He's going to be a big old boy, a six footer.

And I am stronger now than I have ever been in my life. If I am crying (and I try not too) he will know. And he will come into my room and say 'I love you'. And that is enough for me to say 'actually I'll stop crying now'.

He is more like an adult, he is me, a part of me, and I can see so much good in him and he has coped amazingly well without a dad and without male influences in his life. The ones I did bring into his life were awful.

H has good friends. But the thought of him growing up and leaving home scares me.

I have a niece Rebecca and a nephew Ashley, who I love and adore more than anything but unfortunately I don't get to see him as much as I wish I could (Darryl and Dawn's kids) and I wish I could see them more.

But I am so fortunate to have my mum (she is now in her 80s), H, my dogs – and the best friends you could ever imagine.

Me and my friends are 'the three amigos'. It's Jadey, Janey and me.

Since Big Brother I met Jane Brook. While I was in the house Jane and Wanda became avid supporters of me and Rich and they would stick up for us by email on a special forum set up for Big Brother fans. When we left Jane found us on MySpace and we met up. We went to Stringfellows nightclub and got on really well.

Janey is 6ft, blonde and stunning, with legs that go on for six miles – but she hasn't got much confidence because of what men have done to her as well.

We started phoning each other and would meet for dinner or go out clubbing. Jane was going through a really bad part of her life but at least she was lucky enough to have Wanda there for her. I regret I didn't really know Jane well enough at the time to have been there for her like she has been there for me. She has been through hell and back, but come out stronger.

Jane was born with a pure diamond for a heart and there are not many of those people in the world.

All three of us: me Jade and Jane – three separate people from different parts of the country – have so much in common, with our backgrounds in particular, that it's scary. You couldn't separate our backgrounds with a tooth pick.

My friends Jane and Jade Haywood are always there for me. They never question me and I am on the phone to Jane for hours. Not once has she said: "Just shut the fuck up; you are doing my head in."

They let me talk and they will listen. I really am so lucky, so blessed. Friends like them are hard to find. When I am going through hell I know I am not alone, that they're on the end of a phone, and it helps me through, knowing I have the love of my best friends.

And, of all the men to meet, I have recently met a diamond dealer – my 'Mr Diamond'. He is a jewellery designer, a Greek with a heart, body and looks to die for. What more could a girl wish for? They say 'diamonds are a girl's best friend' – no – he is.

I hope we are going to work together in the future, selling his bespoke products to celebrities but no one knows what the future holds.

I first saw Mr Diamond when Janey rang me and told me to have a look at his profile on MySpace (she knew I hadn't had a fella in years). The only men I spoke to were gay ones because I felt comfortable with them. I still didn't trust straight men. How could I after all I had been through?

But I looked at his profile and said: "Crikey, he's fit!"

Jane told me: "He's going to this beauty pageant with us." (Me and Rich were hosting a Queen of Nations transsexual beauty pageant in London – where all the men are absolutely stunning). Our friend Sahara was the organiser.

Rich was with us when I first saw him standing at the bottom of the stairs.

Mr Diamond came and introduced himself and I met him later for a chat – and we spoke for hours and got on really well. Then he rang me and we met up for a drink. And that was it.

I felt comfortable with him straight away; I never felt threatened and never felt he was judging me. He was going through a bad stage in his life at the time and I think I was his shoulder to cry on.

Mr Diamond does not have a bad bone in his body. He is someone with a very pure heart which is hard to find these days. It's nice to be with somebody who is positive all the time, someone who doesn't dwell on the past, someone who looks forward. He's a good bloke and he makes me feel special. Even if we don't make it in the relationship stage, I hope that we will always stay friends and I will always be there for him no matter what – because he is the only man who ever made me comfortable with me being me, and I never felt emotionally or physically threatened – and I just want to thank him for that.

I would like to thank Jane for introducing me to him.

And I would like to thank Mr Diamond for showing me there is good in some men after all.

This year has certainly been very strange in a lot of emotional ways.

In the future I intend to do more work for the BDD Association and for organisations associated with eating disorders. I would love to travel the world for these organisations – to get the message across that it is not something to be ashamed of – that you are not a bad person if you suffer from BDD. That just makes you more individual and special.

And I need to get the message across that you CAN overcome dysmorphia. There are different strains of BDD, some mild, some severe. But at this moment in time I am just so thankful for everything I have and take things day by day.

I am a people person, a people watcher and inquisitive. I like to know about other people's lives and ask questions; that's why I like broadcasting. But my hopes for the future are just to be happy. And if I could plod along with the way my life is at the moment I would be happy.

You never know what's round the corner, what opportunities may arise – or what is going to be taken away. But there's always light at the end of the tunnel no matter how bad life is.

Each day when I wake up I am positive. I don't ever want to wake up again wishing I was dead. Instead I think 'God, I'm lucky to have everything I have got'.

You are a long time dead – so make the most of the time you are here. Try and be optimistic, not a defeatist. Think of good things and good things will happen.

And for those of you suffering from BDD – when you are down, dysmorphia is taking over and you really feel you can't go on because of the hatred you have for yourself – just close your eyes, breathe deeply and think 'I am a good person and I don't deserve to feel this way'. And realise that people around you love you, care for you, and are hurting just as much.

They are powerless to stop you hurting – but you can stop their pain. Give them a smile.

Don't be ashamed of having BDD. It is a condition, like depression, something that happens in the brain. But that does not make you a bad person.

Remember: the best thing in the world for anyone is a cuddle – no matter how rich, poor, happy or sad they are, it's more than money can buy. You can always give someone in need of something a cuddle (or a huggle as Mr Diamond calls it).

And for all the readers out there and for all the people who have BDD, I am giving you the biggest huggle you can ever have – right now.

*You may also enjoy...*

# THE REALITY TELEVISION
## QUIZ BOOK
### 1,000 QUESTIONS ON REALITY TV SHOWS

**COMPILED BY CHRIS COWLIN**
FOREWORD BY CHRISTOPHER BIGGINS